COLOSSIANS

Christ All-sufficient

COLOSSIANS

Christ All-sufficient

by

EVERETT F. HARRISON

MOODY PRESS • CHICAGO

ISBN: 0-8024-2051-6

Library of Congress Catalog Card Number: 76-155694

Printed in the United States of America

CONTENTS

5

INTRODUCTION

As APOSTLE-EVANGELIST, Paul was a founder of churches. As pastor-teacher, he met his responsibility for shepherding these churches by writing to them when he could not visit them in person. Of the various phases of his ministry, the letters affect us most directly, for they continue to speak to us today.

THE LOCATION OF THE COLOSSIAN CHURCH

Usually some knowledge of the community in which a church was situated makes the contents of the letter to that congregation more meaningful. Colosse belonged to southwestern Phrygia, a district of Asia Minor that had been incorporated into the Roman province of Asia in the second century B.C. The city was built along the Lycus River at a point roughly one hundred miles east of Ephesus and enjoyed some commercial importance because of the "Royal Road" running through it, which connected Ephesus in the west with Persia in the east. Nearby were the more prominent cities of Laodicea and Hierapolis (Col 4:13).

Though Christianity became well entrenched in Phrygia, it always had to contend with the people's excitable nature and their tendency to open themselves to novel ideas. Colosse was no exception, judging from Paul's letter.

7

PAUL'S RELATION TO THE CHURCH AT COLOSSE

Though there is a possibility that the apostle may have passed through the place (Ac 19:1), nothing in the letter suggests that he founded the church or was known personally to believers there (Col 1:4; 2:1). Exceptions are Philemon (Phile 1), whose slave Onesimus belonged to Colosse (Col 4:9), and Epaphras, who seems to have been the one who established the church (Col 1:6-7). It is likely that both men visited Ephesus while Paul ministered there; and after being instructed in the faith by him they became active in evangelizing their local area (cf. Ac 19:10).

In view of this rather indirect connection with the Colossian church, Paul's pastoral concern for the congregation is remarkable. Compared to Romans, likewise written to a church he did not establish personally, Colossians is more intimate. Paul shows great solicitude for his readers and shares with them his own labors, trials, and longings (e.g., 1:24, 28-29; 2:1, 5; 4:3-4, 7-9, 15-18).

AUTHORSHIP OF COLOSSIANS

A good starting point is the observation that there are obvious ties between this letter and Philemon. About the latter, no serious question can be raised as to its Pauline authorship. From Colossians 4:7-9 it is evident that Paul is sending two men to Colosse: Tychicus, the bearer of the Colossian letter, and Onesimus, whose mission is clearly indicated in the letter to Philemon. Archippus is mentioned in both communications (Col 4:17; Phile 2). Furthermore, Paul's companions are the same in both: Mark, Aristarchus, Demas, and Luke (Phile 24; Col 4:10, 14).

One need not be disturbed because there are some words

in Colossians which do not appear in Paul's other writings. Every letter he wrote has some terms peculiar to it. Nor should one be alarmed because the heresy Paul combats here seems to resemble somewhat a second century movement known as Gnosticism. The resemblances are offset by the differences. Colossians clearly belongs to the first century. This is discussed further in the last section of this chapter.

OCCASION AND PURPOSE

In some way Paul has learned of tendencies in the Colossian church that need correction. Whether this information came by letter cannot be determined. Epaphras, who was with Paul at the time of writing, is most naturally thought of as the informant. True, Paul accents the positive side of Epaphras' report (1:8), but there is at least a hint of distress in another allusion (4:12). It is understandable that Paul might hesitate to picture his friend as an informer and thus endanger the latter's influence among some elements of the congregation.

From the letter itself it becomes obvious that Paul faithfully goes about the task of exposing false teaching. But it becomes equally obvious that the apostle is not content merely to combat error. He feels the obligation to build up his readers in the faith (1:28), whether by prayer (1:9-14) or instruction (2:9-15) or exhortation (3:1-10).

PLACE OF COMPOSITION

Paul is in prison at the time of writing (4:10, 18). But where? Three places have been suggested: Caesarea, Ephesus, and Rome. The first is unlikely because in Philemon

22 Paul asks that a lodging be prepared for him. He evidently hopes for release and plans a trip to Colosse. At this very time he wrote Colossians. However, there was nothing in the apostle's situation at Caesarea to encourage a hope for release (Ac 24:24-27) ; and in all probability he still expected to go on to Rome as soon as possible (19:21; 20:38). The Lord had not cancelled His assuring word that His servant would bear a testimony on His behalf in the imperial city (23:11). Once Paul's appeal had been made to Caesar, he was under the necessity of going to Rome for trial (26:32).

The second suggestion (Ephesus) suffers from lack of clear evidence that Paul was imprisoned there. Further, Luke is with him at the time of writing (Col 4:14), yet apparently was not with him in Ephesus. At least the account of Paul's ministry there lacks the use of *we* which emerges in other places where Luke indicates in this way his presence with the apostle (Ac 16:10 ff.; 20:6, 13 ff.; 27:1 ff.).

Rome, then, remains the most likely place. Luke made the sea journey with Paul (Ac 27:1), so it is natural to think of him as continuing to be with Paul through this time of stress preceding the trial. The close of Acts relates that the apostle was obliged to wait at least two years for this event. During that time, by letter and through friends, he was able to maintain communication with the churches.

DATE

Paul's stay in Rome is best put early in the sixties; and a probable time for Colossians is the year 62, which is an

approximation rather than a precise date. A somewhat
earlier date is possible.

RELATION OF COLOSSIANS TO EPHESIANS

That these two letters have a close affinity is evident to
any observant reader. Both were carried by the same messenger (Col 4:7-8; Eph 6:21-22). Both are greatly occupied
with Christ and the church, which in Ephesians is viewed
mostly in the universal rather than in the local sense. In
Colossians the term *body* is preferred to *church*. Both letters magnify the headship of Christ over the body, but
Colossians puts special emphasis on His supremacy in the
cosmos, a truth not completely lacking from Ephesians
(1:10, 21-22; 4:10). Both mention angelic powers. But,
whereas Colossians was designed to meet the challenge of
false teaching, Ephesians was written for spiritual edification. Many words, phrases, and even sentences are the same
in both, suggesting that the two documents were written
with only a brief interval between them.

THE FALSE TEACHING IN THE CHURCH

The reader of Galatians does not experience much diffi-
culty in determining the error Paul is combating there. But
in Colossians references to the problem are less direct and
less sharply stated, so the exact nature of the Colossian
heresy remains somewhat elusive. Paul deals with it in
chapters 1 and 2—in the former section using the positive
approach of exalting Christ in the uniqueness of His person and work, and in the latter portion using at times the
technique of warning and correction.

It is not easy for moderns to capture the thought-world

in which most people lived in the Graeco-Roman civilization of Paul's day. The heyday of Greek philosophy had
passed. Men were still given to speculation about the
universe and human life but hardly with the acumen and
logic of the masters who preceded them. The boldness
born of curiosity that characterized the classical period had
given way to what has been called a failure of nerve. It
was an age of fear and superstition. Man's place in the
universe was insecure. The heavenly bodies were often
thought of as affecting the welfare and destiny of human
beings, being associated with deities or powerful spirits
that could make life miserable and even interfere with the
attainment of heavenly bliss in the life to come. By superior knowledge or perchance by magical manipulation one
might be able to cancel the efforts of these powers who had
hostile intent, especially if he gave himself to the adoration
of angels who were in position to help him. Underlying
this outlook was the characteristic Greek notion of the
opposition between spirit and matter. Man's hope lay in
an ultimate spirit existence free from the grip of life in
the body, which was depreciated as basically evil. Mean-
while it was to his advantage to regulate his life with some
care, denying bodily appetites as a means of purification.
If by mystical contemplation he could manage a visionary
experience, it might be possible for him actually to rise
above earthly limitations and eventually to be absorbed
into the life enjoyed by the gods.

Ideas of this nature formed the substance of much of the
popular religion of Paul's day. Instead of maintaining
loyalty to one god or to one system of thought in exclusive
fashion, men felt free to borrow various notions and prac-

tices. If one avenue should prove to be a dead end, another might be more promising. This policy in itself was an admission of uncertainty and desperation.

The dominant outlook, as noted, was dualistic, viewing the realm of the divine and the world of man as separated by a wide gap. A few decades after Paul's time, in the second century, the system of thought known as Gnosticism became fully developed, with a doctrine of a series of angelic beings forming a kind of ladder, those nearest God being the most free from evil and those nearest the world being the most contaminated. One had to know how to make use of these mediating beings to escape from the bonds of material existence into the realm of light where the soul could enjoy release. Gnosticism, as the root word *gnosis* suggests, emphasized knowledge as the key to deliverance from the hold of evil.

In the first century, however, Gnosticism was not fully developed; so even though certain gnostic catchwords appear in Colossians, it is doubtful that they have the technical force which they came to have later on. For example, there is no evidence that *plēroma* (fullness) is used with the same meaning it had in Gnosticism, where it denoted the sum of the higher aeons to which the soul must work its way by successfully contending with the lower powers that are tinctured with evil.

Consequently, if Gnosticism is to be considered as the Colossian heresy, it must be with the qualification that it is an undeveloped, early form of this type of religious thought.

It seems evident from the letter that there were Jewish elements also in the system that threatened to make in-

roads into the Colossian church. This comes to the fore
especially in 2:16, where Paul shows his awareness that
attempts are being made to convince the saints that they
ought to observe the Levitical code regarding clean and
unclean foods, and to keep the Sabbath and the Jewish
festivals. Jewish influence may account also for the worship of angels (2:18). If the epistle to the Hebrews was
written to Jewish Christians, which is highly probable,
then the fact that its first two chapters are devoted largely
to showing the superiority of God's Son to all these heavenly creatures can be taken as evidence that this tendency was
already present among its readers. Doubtless the Jewish
veneration for the Mosaic Law fostered such regard for
angels, seeing that they were reputed to have had a part
in mediating the law to Israel (Heb 2:2; Ac 7:53; Gal
3:19).

Jewish thought of the sectarian type found in the writings of the Qumran community may have an echo here and
there in Colossians not only with regard to the place
accorded to angelic beings but also in reference to the flesh,
the terminology of light and darkness, the observance of
the Sabbath, a tendency to asceticism, and the like. But
not all the distinctives of Qumran are reflected in Colossians; therefore, if it be true that influences from this sect
had penetrated to Colosse, only fragments of Qumran
thought and practice had affected the group to whom Paul
wrote.

In a sense, heresy is a testimony to the vitality of the
Christian faith, for the very fact that men seek to improve
on it shows that they cannot ignore it. Examination of this
letter by Paul makes evident that each aspect of the false

teaching has its answer in Christ, in whom the fullness of divine life, wisdom, and power resides. Christ is the believer's sufficiency (Col 2:9-10; 3:3-4).

In view of the fact that Colossians was written largely to meet a theological aberration, it is not surprising that Paul should emphasize from the start the truth of the gospel (1:5, 23) and the faith to which Christians adhere (1:23; 2:7), thus calling attention to the standard that unites believers everywhere. Quite naturally, too, in meeting the challenge of error, the apostle refuses to concede that knowledge is the special possession of the errorists. Knowledge, wisdom, and understanding are part of the believer's inheritance in Christ.

There is no likelihood that the teachers of this "philosophy" went so far as to deny that the fullness of God dwelt in Christ and thus make Him less than truly divine; for, if they had taken this position, we may be sure that the apostle would have spoken out much more directly and severely. His point is that in Christ *all* the fullness of deity has its abode (Col 2:9). This leaves no room for the fullness to be shared in some measure with other beings.

The most dangerous heresies the church is called on to combat from time to time are not those which openly and blatantly assail the person of our Lord but rather those which subtly detract from His dignity while giving the appearance of honoring Him. Those who perceive this danger will always treasure Colossians as a manual for exposing points of view which have many good things to say about the head of the church but proceed to dim the luster of His glory by eclipsing His preeminence. There would be limited value in this book if Paul had been content merely to issue a string of denials of the false teaching which had been made known to him. But, in the process of meeting error, the apostle was led to give us deep insights into the person and work of our Saviour, preeminent over all personages and forces, unique in His redeeming and reconciling ministry for mankind, the head of the church whose risen life flows into all the members of His body; and thus the message has abundant appeal for successive generations of believers.

OUTLINE OF COLOSSIANS

1

INTRODUCTION OF THE EPISTLE

1:1-14

GREETING TO THE CHURCH (1:1-2)

IN THE MATTER OF FORM, the apostle's letters show considerable similarity to secular communications of a personal sort from that era; but even so they include a Christian note (v. 2) that sets them apart from ordinary letters.

To his name Paul adds his position in the church of Christ. Yet his rank of *apostle* was not bestowed by the church or by any individual (Gal 1:1). He was called into the service of the Lord *by the will of God* (cf. 1 Co 1:1; 2 Co 1:1), which rules out any suggestion that he himself had aspired to this place of leadership. His reference to apostleship does not necessarily indicate that any challenge to his standing had been raised at Colosse, but rather he wishes to make known at the very beginning that he is Christ's representative and as such is fully qualified to deal with matters discussed in the body of the letter.

His designation of the Saviour as "Christ Jesus" (the reading of the leading manuscripts) may be understood as a deliberate effort to emphasize at the very outset the

present exalted position of the risen Lord over against a
system of thought which tended to rob Him of His full
majesty. Paul does not use the name *Jesus* alone in this
letter.

"Timothy our brother" is included in the greeting. This
is true of all the captivity letters except Ephesians, where
all mention of other individuals is omitted, presumably
because of the general or encyclical nature of the communication. In fact, the name of this close companion and
valued helper appears, joined with Paul's, in most of the
apostle's writings. *Brother* never ceased to be richly meaningful to Paul since the day he heard it coupled with his
own name and spoken by a man he had intended to per-
secute (Ac 9:17).

The recipients of the letter are noted as being in residence at Colosse but also as being *in Christ,* a far more
significant position than their location on the map. In
their relation to God they are *saints,* or "set-apart ones,"
belonging to Him who called them and therefore charged
with reflecting His holy character in their lives. In their
relation to each other they are *brethren* who can also be
called *faithful.* Although this latter term can mean "believing" (full of faith), to render it so here would be virtually meaningless, since *brethren* implies a believing relationship to Christ. By pronouncing his readers "faithful,"
Paul may be expressing his confidence that, when he has
shown them the peril of being influenced by wrong teaching, they will turn away from it. The simple reminder that
they are "in Christ" should serve to spur their fidelity to
the One who has become the center of their lives and their
hope for the age to come. As a help to them they have also

an example of faithfulness in the ministry of Epaphras (Col 1:7).

Instead of extending a conventional greeting such as an unbeliever might use, Paul desires for his readers a fresh supply of divine "grace and peace" and a fresh realization of what these mean. *Grace* naturally has the priority, for apart from grace no acceptance with God would be possible. When grace meets with the response of faith, peace results. The sinner is no longer at enmity with God, and his life takes on wholeness and soundness as he rests in the assurance of divine favor.

THANKSGIVING FOR THE COLOSSIAN CHRISTIANS (1:3-8)

Such a thanksgiving is usual in Paul's letters to churches, although the "blessed be God" formula is used in 2 Corinthians and Ephesians. No thanksgiving appears in Galatians, where Paul pours out instead his anguish and disappointment over the defection of some of his converts.

Having given expression here in Colossians to his own gratitude to God, the apostle rightfully can call upon his readers to have the same response; and this he does repeatedly (Col 1:12; 2:7; 3:15, 17; 4:2).

"We give thanks to God." Is Timothy being included here? Probably so, in view of the contrast with Philippians 1:3, where Paul does not use the plural, even though Timothy's name is joined with his at the beginning. Prayer for these Christians at Colosse must be accompanied with gratitude to God on every occasion, for the reason that the primary virtues of *faith* and *love* are not lacking in them. *Faith* belongs to them in the sphere of Christ Jesus. It focused on Him at the inception of their spiritual experience, and now it permeates their entire relationship to God. Faith is the root of Christian life, and love is the fruit. In this case Paul is thankful that love is not concentrated on a few but reaches out to include "all the saints," which at the very least must mean all believers in Colosse and conceivably could mean Christians everywhere (cf. Eph 3:18). In several of Paul's writings, faith and love occur in coordination (1 Th 3:6; 2 Th 1:3; Phile 5; cf. Eph 6:23).

At times *hope* is added as the third of the primary virtues (1 Th 1:3; 1 Co 13:13). Such might seem to be the case here, since hope is included almost immediately (Col 1:5). Yet it stands somewhat apart; and the whole statement is difficult to grasp, especially in the King James Version.* Even the rendering, "because of the hope laid up for you in heaven" (Revised Standard Version†) calls for explanation. It is probably best understood as looking back to the faith and love. What is so astonishing is the suggestion that faith and love, which are exercised here and now, are dependent on the hope which relates to the future. But hope creates an anticipation in the heart that has a powerful effect upon present attitudes. The prospect of being with other believers in the presence of Christ for all eternity makes the fellowship of love in this life all the more meaningful. Paul goes on to say that hope is part of the gospel message and that the Colossians are familiar with the glorious inheritance awaiting the saints (cf. 1:12).

The word of the truth of the gospel is closely parallel to a similar statement in Ephesians 1:13. If the gospel were not

*Hereafter cited as KJV.
†Hereafter cited as RSV.

true, it would not be good news but only cruel deception. It is just possible that here the apostle is glancing by way of contrast at the error which is current at Colosse, which he is soon to attack openly in his letter. In his other controversial epistle he twice refers to the truth of the gospel (Gal 2:5, 14). The best way to deal with error is to hold it up to the light of truth which God has revealed.

Since his readers have heard the message before, he does not have to spell out the gospel, though he will refer to aspects of it from time to time in his exposition. Here he is content to make the point that the very same message which has come to the people in Colosse has reached to others "in all the world" (Col 1:6). Paul had personally carried it to both east and west. But this language is not intended as a missionary boast. J. B. Lightfoot is helpful here: "More lurks under these words than appears on the surface. The true Gospel, the Apostle seems to say, proclaims its truth by its universality. The false gospels are the outgrowths of local circumstances, of special idiosyncrasies; the true Gospel is the same everywhere. The false gospels address themselves to limited circles; the true Gospel proclaims itself boldly throughout the world. Heresies are at best ethnic; truth is essentially catholic."[1]

But Paul is not content to appeal only to the widespread reception of the truth, as though numbers of adherents could be construed as a guarantee of the truth of the message. He passes to a second consideration. The gospel invites comparison from the standpoint of its effectiveness—"bearing fruit and increasing" (American Standard Version*). The truth makes a difference; it transforms lives.

*Hereafter cited as ASV.

By these two observations the apostle adroitly prepares the way for his frontal assault on the Colossian heresy. He is suggesting that true Christianity carries credentials which false teaching cannot equal.

However, the apostle has not quite finished his initial preparation. He reserves to the last the great distinctive of the gospel: the fact that it enshrines the *grace of God*. All other religions proceed on the assumption that man must commend himself to God, or, as in the case of the Galatian error, that a mixture of human effort with divine grace is required. By a simple mention of God's grace this early in the letter, coupled with the reminder that his readers have come to know the meaning of that grace as a reality in their lives, Paul is already laying the axe to the root of legalism that he will tear out later and cast aside before the eyes of the Colossians (Col 2:16-23).

In these preliminary observations the apostle sounds an optimistic note, for he comments that the gospel is producing fruit among his readers (Col 1:6) as truly as elsewhere. This suggests his confidence, based on the information he has, that the bulk of the Christian community remains sound. They are not a diseased plant. Their fruit testifies to their spiritual health.

Now, at the close of the paragraph, Epaphras comes into view, presented from two standpoints: first as the one who has faithfully taught the gospel in Colosse (v. 7), and then as the source of Paul's information about believers in that city. In fact, we must go back to the close of verse 6 to pick up the two words *in truth* in order to follow Paul's train of thought. From the lips of this man who founded the church, nothing was heard but the pure gospel. Believers were started along the right path. Paul states the relationship of this brother to himself in terms of a "dear fellow-servant," and his relationship to Christ as a "faithful minister." Should a Christian worker desire any higher commendation?

An interesting problem is bound up with these words of praise. According to the KJV, Paul describes Epaphras as one "who is for you a faithful minister of Christ." This reads well and makes sense. But there is good manuscript authority for a slightly different wording—*us* instead of *you*. If this be accepted as the true text—and it strongly commends itself—then the thought is that Paul regards Epaphras as his substitute, his alter ego, who has carried out a mission which Paul would have delighted to accomplish but was unable to carry out. As the leading apostle to the Gentiles, he considered Colosse a legitimate part of his mission field; but since he could not go everywhere, he was glad to send men who knew the Word and would declare it faithfully.

So much for what Epaphras has told the Colossians. But what has he told Paul, now that he has come to him at Rome? He has reported their "love in the Spirit." Doubtless in the first instance this means love for one another, but it would naturally include Paul, the teacher of the one who had come to mean so much to them. Yet Paul, with his usual delicacy, will not lay claim to any special consideration. This solitary reference to the Spirit in this book is highly appropriate, for love is the primary fruit of the Spirit (Gal 5:22). Paul is talking, then, about something more than a merely human sentiment. It is the love of Christ reproduced by the Spirit in the lives of His people.

PRAYER FOR THE READERS (1:9-14)

The prayer follows commendation of a high order. Faith and love are present, and Paul has given thanks for this. Evidently, then, it is not because the believers are deficient in such matters that Paul now prays for them. The prayer itself provides the answer. As Bishop Moule remarks, "The state in which they are has inevitably, with its blessings, its risks also. It is the very state in which a lack of direction may bring loss, if not disaster. The sails are set so full that the need of compass and rudder is the more pressing."[2] This comment is sustained by the way the apostle introduces his prayer: "for this cause," which looks backward to the thanksgiving.

Paul's prayer life never ceases to amaze us. Here he affirms that he has not ceased to pray for the Colossians since he heard of their spiritual state. Let it not be said that the explanation can be found in his situation—a prisoner with time on his hands. Even when he was busily engaged in ministering to the growing church in Corinth, he could write to the Thessalonians that he was remembering them in unceasing prayer (1 Th 1:3). Perhaps there is a relationship between the time devoted to prayer and the quality of the prayer that results. In Colossians and the other epistles of the captivity in Rome the apostle's prayers have ripened to their full maturity and are fully abreast of the exalted teaching with which they are interspersed.

Knowledge seems to be the key thought of this prayer (vv. 9-10). In this respect it closely resembles the prayer

in Ephesians 1:17-19. It is in the area of spiritual perception that the Colossians stand in need of help. Without it
they can easily be victimized by a system of thought that
could devitalize their whole Christian experience. Their
precarious condition is the reason why the apostle is not
content to say simply that he is praying for these people.
He wants them to know *what* he is praying for.

His concern is not different from that of Epaphras (Col
4:12). It has to do with the knowledge of God's *will* and
a life lived in accordance with that will. As we know, Jesus
was supremely concerned with the will of God (Jn 4:34;
6:38; Lk 22:42). Paul's conversion and mission revolved
around the same thing (Ac 22:14-15). God's will centers
in His plan of salvation for the children of men and all
that is involved in executing that plan.

The knowledge of God's will requires "all wisdom and
spiritual understanding." These are not to be thought of
as man's native capacities but as gifts of the Spirit, as the
word *spiritual* clearly indicates (cf. v. 8). Wisdom is
referred to six times in this epistle, which means a heavy
emphasis, considering the brevity of the writing, and is to
be understood in the light of the problem facing the
church. Divine enlightenment is needed to separate truth
from error. False teaching may have an appearance of wisdom and yet be quite contrary to divine revelation. It is
especially at the focal point of the cross that human and
divine wisdom show their great divergence (1 Co 1:23-
24). The biblical idea of wisdom links it closely with goodness; so that, when this is lacking, the word takes on an
ironical twist. So, for example, the word *philosophy*, which
Paul uses in Colossians 2:8 with reference to false teaching,

sounds quite harmless when it is translated literally as "love of wisdom." But it easily degenerates into a passion to know something for the sake of knowing it; and when this knowledge is regarded as superior to what the rank and file possess, it inevitably leads to pride.

The kind of wisdom Paul seeks for the Colossians is transcendently practical, for it is intended to enable the child of God to "walk worthy of the Lord unto all pleasing" (v. 10). This combination of walking and pleasing brings to mind the case of Enoch, the man who walked with God and who, before being taken to be with Him, was attested as being pleasing to Him (Heb 11:5). *Walking* implies both direction and progress—knowing the will of God and increasing in the performance of it. If Paul had any ambition that topped any other, it was this, that he might be well pleasing to the Lord Christ (2 Co 5:9). What he desired for himself he desired also for his Christian friends.

The life that pleases the Lord is the fruitful life, abounding "in every good work." Without cultivation there can be no harvest. We are accustomed to think of future reward in connection with work done for the Lord, and this is true enough; but the great surprise is the present reward— "increasing in the knowledge of God." Here is the sequence: seeking to be well pleasing to the Lord, demonstrating this desire in active fruitbearing, receiving the result of increased knowledge of God. In other words, the way to extend our knowledge of God is to seek to please Him by working out in practice what is revealed to us as His will. The secret of the Lord is with them that fear Him and obey Him.

Just as there is need of wisdom for the walk, so there is

need of *power* for the endurance of the believer in situations which call for more than human resources can supply. *Patience* (Endurance, RSV) means bearing up under trial, refusing to buckle under the pressure. *Longsuffering* is the patient spirit that takes all the abuse without blowing up. It is to the glory of God to make this kind of power available to His people, so that they are victorious under trial, as Jesus was in the days of His flesh. Endurance and longsuffering are tremendous assets; but when they are accompanied by *joyfulness,* they reveal their supernatural character. Again it is the life of Christ lived over again in His people that comes shining through (cf. Heb 12:2).

Joyfulness and thankfulness are partners (Col 1:12). It is hard to conceive of one without the other. If there is joy in the midst of suffering, there is also thankfulness for the privilege of enduring for Christ's sake. Incidentally, error has very little chance of making inroads upon a life that is gratefully exuberant in Christ (*see* Phil 3:1-3).

The expression of thanksgiving extends over three verses (Col 1:12-14). In the first, thanksgiving is directed to the Father; in the second, both Father and Son are mentioned; in the third, the Son alone. God the Father, as the sovereign Lord of history, had wrought mightily in behalf of His chosen people Israel, providing them an inheritance in the land of Canaan and giving the tribes their individual portions by lot. The whole procedure was calculated to remind them that they were dependent on His power and lovingkindness for everything. So with the Christian. God has sufficed us to have a share with other saints in the heavenly inheritance which awaits us. Paul could trace this truth about an "inheritance of the saints" to his call from the risen Lord (Ac 26:18). What has been reserved for believers is a realm of *light* (*see* Rev 22:5).

It is possible that the Old Testament background continues to influence the thought as the thanksgiving takes in deliverance from the power of darkness (Col 1:13). One of the plagues visited on Egypt, the house of bondage, was darkness (Ex 10:21-23); and the pillar of cloud was darkness to the Egyptian hosts and light to the children of Israel (Ex 14:20). It was only God's power that *delivered* His people from their plight. As He transferred them into Canaan, so has He *translated* believers into the kindom of the Son of His love. This *kingdom* has a present reality for New Testament saints, for the transfer has taken place already. It is described by Paul elsewhere as meaning "righteousness, and peace, and joy in the Holy Ghost" (Ro 14:17). Jesus was obliged to come under the power of darkness in the very process of delivering us from it (Lk 22:53)

We would be entirely unfit for the kingdom were it not for the *redemption* procured for us at the cross by God's Son. The initial benefit of this redemption is the *forgiveness of sins*. As the parallel passage in Ephesians 1:7 reminds us, this blessed result was made possible through the blood of Christ shed in behalf of sinners. In the day of Christ, at His coming, redemption will be provided for the body (Ro 8:23), which will complete our salvation (Phil 3:20-21). It is then that saints will enter upon their inheritance about which Paul has spoken in verse 12, and the difference between the darkness of Satan's kingdom and the heavenly kingdom of light and righteousness will become fully manifest.

2

THE PERSON AND WORK OF CHRIST

1:15-29

In Creation and Redemption (1:15-20)

Two basic thoughts predominate in this passage. First, God's Son, who is described as the image of the invisible God, is set forth as the agent in creation and as the head of the church. The relation to God is not developed, but enough is given to establish the fact of His deity. Next His twofold work is unfolded: first in creation, then in redemption.

The connection with the preceding verses is close, as Christ continues to be the subject; and the thought, after briefly taking in His relation to God and then to the creation, returns to the theme of redemption which the apostle has made prominent at the close of his prayer.

Some students have thought that these verses are of hymnic mold, and largely on this basis they have suggested that Paul may have taken over something already in existence and adapted it to his purpose. But this conclusion is speculative. It may be granted that the ideas expressed were not peculiar to Paul but were shared with others in the church. He does not introduce them as a fresh revelation given to himself on this occasion.

The lofty Christology of this passage stands in striking contrast to Paul's preconversion view of Jesus of Nazareth. From the time of his confrontation with the risen Lord on the Damascus road, he had to reckon with the fact of the resurrection. As surely as this great event pointed forward to the glorious consummation, it also demanded an appraisal of the person of Christ in terms of His eternal and preincarnate dignity. The self-revelation of the Lord to His own, plus His unfolding of the Old Testament disclosures about Him, no doubt provided the church with the necessary data for such a portrayal as that of the present passage. Even so, the ascended Christ is chiefly in view.

He is "the image of the invisible God" (v. 15). The word *image* goes beyond the idea of similarity, suggesting exact reproduction. Nothing of God is lacking in the person of His Son. We must not be misled by His subordination to the Father into the assumption that He was actually an inferior being. Paul uses the term *image* in reference to Christ in 2 Corinthians 4:4 also (cf. *"express* image," Heb 1:3). Closely related is the Pauline affirmation that Christ was in the form of God (Phil 2:6), which has to do with essential being rather than appearance.

Something else is suggested by the word *invisible;* namely, that whereas God, by virtue of His spiritual nature (Jn 1:18; 4:24; 1 Ti 6:16) must remain unseen to His creatures, yet the revelation of Himself is possible through the One who bears the stamp of His being and nature. In the world to come, the Lord Jesus will continue to be the revelation of the invisible God to the redeemed.

With this brief word about the Son's relation to God, the apostle passes immediately to another thought. The revealer of God is also "the firstborn of all creation" (ASV). This is not an easy statement to comprehend. A good starting point is the word *firstborn*. It is used of Jesus in relation to Mary His mother (Lk 2:7). That other children followed seems to be implied. Even so, the idea of distinction, of uniqueness may be implied here. Certainly that is the usual force of the word. The nation Israel was God's firstborn (Ex 4:22), and clearly no other was intended to follow. So in the passage before us, the principal emphasis falls on Christ's sovereignty. He is first in the sense of being preeminent (cf. Col 1:18). Yet the problem remains that the statement seems on the surface to make Christ a part of creation. But no such thing could have been intended by Paul, for we go on to read that, instead of being created, He was the Creator and was before all things (vv. 16-17). So His relation to the creation is not that of being brought into being but standing above it as its Maker. *In* Him the creation finds its source and explanation. Likewise, *through* Him all things were created, for He was the instrument by which the universe was brought into being. Finally, all things were created *for* Him. This in itself is sufficient to silence any claims that Christ as the firstborn is less than God. If creation has its goal in Him, then He must be absolutely and without qualification true and eternal deity.

Looking at the body of the verse, one cannot fail to be impressed by the fact that Paul begins to describe the creation in terms familiar to the reader of the Old Testament (Gen 1:1). But rather than elaborate on the creation of the *earth*, Paul proceeds to draw out the implications of the creation of *heaven*. He passes by any enlargement on things *visible* and expands instead on the *invisible*. The reason is evident. Angels had a certain fascination for some of the Colossians, and the error in their midst advocated the adoration of these celestial beings (Col 2:18). Paul begins early to put them in a place of inferiority to Christ, who created them (cf. Heb 1:2-4).

Several descriptive terms are used for these angelic beings. They do not seem to be arranged in any observable hierarchy, but the very fact that the plural *thrones* is used is significant. No one of these creatures has a solitary throne such as the Almighty occupies, which He shares with the Son (Heb 1:7-8). That Paul was prepared to concede that angelic beings of great authority exist is beyond question, for it would be idle to tell believers that their wrestling is not against flesh and blood but against principalities and powers (Eph 6:12) if these had no real existence. Since the passage in Ephesians makes clear that some, at least, of these heavenly intelligences are bent on doing harm to the Christian cause, the question is naturally forced upon us as to what sort of beings the apostle is describing in Colossians 1:16. It is wise to take the comprehensive view—angels whether good or bad, loyal or fallen. In the light of Christ's preeminence, the help of good angels need not be sought and the hurt of evil angels need not be feared.

Twice the apostle insists in this one verse that all things were created in and through Christ. But the second statement goes beyond the first, since the tense of the verb takes in not merely the act of creation but glances at the status quo which the creation imposes on all who are a part of it. The angelic orders have their bounds, even as the sea and land. No angelic being can supplant the Creator. An angel of superlative beauty and power seems to have tried it, only to end up as Satan, the adversary, doomed to ultimate failure and judgment.

"He is before all things" (v. 17). Christ naturally antedated all that He brought into being. Conscious in the days of His earthly existence of His preincarnate state, He could with all seriousness make the staggering claim, "Before Abraham was, I am" (Jn 8:58). "By him all things consist" ("hold together," RSV). The universe is definitely personal. His power upholds and guides what His hands have wrought. All the elements cohere in Him. As Bishop Moule put it, "He is their Bond, their Order, their Law."[1]

The apostle does not linger to draw out the implications of this sweeping statement but passes at once to another area of Christ's unique supremacy. "He is the head of the body, the church" (Col 1:18). This means that the Lord has a dual headship, taking in both the creation and the church. The drawing together of these two roles has tremendous significance for us, tending to personalize our view of the universe, since the Maker of all things is none other than our Saviour and our Friend. Again, the close coordination of the two headships opens the way for the unifying of theology and science. There is no sharp separation in the mind of Christ between the natural order and the spiritual, for He is responsible for both. As His people we can be at home in both. Control over the creation belongs to Christ, for He made it; and control over the church is His because of the redemption He has achieved by His death (v. 20), of which His resurrection is a testimony and ground of assurance (v. 18).

The term *head* denotes both superiority and authority. Elsewhere Paul asserts the headship of Christ over the individual man (1 Co 11:3); here he stresses the corporate relationship. Sometimes the apostle makes use of the figure of the body to emphasize the varied nature of the members and their mutual need of one another, but here he is concerned to press home the truth that the body necessarily depends on its head. Both Christ's authority and His wisdom, along with His life and power, are communicated to those who serve Him to make an impact on the life of the world.

Important as the church is, Paul refuses to be sidetracked into a discussion of it, such as he provides in Ephesians; for he is intent on magnifying Christ Himself. For the fourth time we are told that *He is*. The Lord put forth His greatest claims by means of the formula "I am." In its response the church believingly asserts, "He is" (e.g., Ac 10:36).

We feel a certain abruptness in the statement that He is *the beginning* and are inclined to ask, "The beginning of what?" Hardly the beginning or source of the creation, for that has been covered. The remainder of the verse provides the needed guidance, suggesting that Christ's relation to the church, the new creation, is in view. Elsewhere He is called the Prince of life (Ac 3:15) and the Captain of salvation (Heb 2:10). The same word translated "beginning" in Colossians 1:18 is a part of the term that is used for both of these titles. The idea imparted is that of one who makes a start, who opens a way for others to follow. Christ initiates salvation, opening the way to the Father and granting power to those who follow Him in the path-

way of obedience. It can be seen readily that time is not
of the essence in this use of *beginning*.

The same is true of "the firstborn from the dead," for the
dominant thought is supremacy over the realm of death.
He left the dead when He came forth from their midst in
the power of His resurrection. Paul does not say here, as
in 1 Corinthians 15:20, that the risen Lord is the firstfruits
of those who sleep in death, though that truth might
readily be inferred from his statement. What he main-
tains are Christ's victory over death in His own person and
His resultant right to institute a new creation into which
death cannot penetrate with its gloomy grip (cf. Rev 5:9-
10). By His resurrection our Lord attained the place of
preeminence over all things. The resurrection was a tremendous demonstration of power (Ro 1:4; Eph 1:19-23),
followed as it was by His ascension and session at the right
hand of the throne of God. True, He has not yet extended
His rule over all things, but He has the authority to do so
as He awaits the appropriate time.

In moving on to verse 19, it is well to note that the word
for establishes a close connection in thought with what precedes. Evidently *all fulness* is intimately related to preeminence. By comparing this expression with 2:9 it is possible to conclude that the deity of Christ is intended here,
and this accords with the idea of preeminence. No angelic
beings rank with Him, and for this reason none deserve to
share in that fullness. They are entirely subordinate to
Him.

The word *dwell* is a strong term, meaning to abide completely and permanently.

But a problem remains. Unless something is added

(KJV supplies "the Father"), the construction of the verse
appears to require that "all fulness" was pleased to dwell
in Christ. But if this is the actual intent of the apostle,
then the fullness must also be the subject of the following
sentence and be represented as making peace through the
reconciling work of Christ at the cross. But elsewhere Paul
makes God the author of reconciliation through Christ
(2 Co 5:18-19). So it is wise to conclude that Paul is thinking of the Father as purposing all this—the dwelling of full
deity in the Son and the reconciling of all things to Himself. The situation was such that only God could provide
in Himself, that is, within the Godhead, the solution to the
tragedy of a lost and estranged creation.

The mention of *peace* (v. 20) implies a state of enmity
for which *the blood* of Christ was the solution. "He is our
peace" (Eph 2:14). But whereas in Ephesians the apostle's
thought has a twofold character—the removal of enmity
between men and God, and between Jews and Gentiles—
only the former is discussed here in Colossians. Some dif-
ficulty is created by the fact that the purpose of God in
reconciliation is said to embrace "all things." Does this
mean that the animal and inanimate creation must be
thought of as included? Hardly, because there is no enmity
toward God in these areas; and without enmity there is no
need of reconciliation. In the Greek language the neuter
plural *all things* can be used to express universality within
the universe of discourse demanded by the context. Here
Paul supplies a context by including *earth* and *heaven*.
Then heavenly as well as earthly beings are embraced in
the scope of reconciliation. Because of what Christ has
done, in the new heaven and earth only righteousness can

dwell. His reconciling work will prove as far-reaching as
His creative activity (v. 16). The precise meaning of reconciliation for things in heaven is elusive. It would be
hazardous to think of rebellious angels. Perhaps loyal
angels are in view, placed beyond the possibility of defection in the future.

IN RELATION TO THE COLOSSIANS (1:21-23)

No longer speaking in sweeping generalities, the apostle
turns to his readers, "and you," to remind them that they
were alienated and enemies in their attitude toward God.
That attitude was reflected in their "wicked works." Most
men refrain from shaking their fists at the Almighty,
whether from fear of reprisal or from the feeling that their
fellows would disapprove; yet the underlying hostility to
Him is shown in their disregard of His commandments and
the stifling of conscience. "Yet now hath he reconciled"—
even in the face of rebellion and bitter hatred, God carried
through the work of reconciliation. He took the initiative,
without waiting for men to come halfway. It is God who
acts in reconciliation; it is man who is reconciled.

How did God go about it? In the person of His Son, so
that Christ can be represented as reconciling (cf. 2 Co
5:19). It took place "in the body of his flesh [and] through
[His] death" (Col 1:22). There can be no doubt that the
language is designed deliberately to counteract the false
spiritualism advanced by the error that threatened the
church. That false spiritualism maintained that no being
possessed of a material body could possibly accomplish
reconciliation to a deity who was pure spirit. The angels
qualified at this point, and Jesus Christ did not. But the

stubborn fact of history had to be emphasized. The Son of God had come in the *flesh* (Jn 1:14), had lived His life on earth in the flesh (Heb 5:7), and in the flesh had offered Himself on the cross as an offering for sin. The wages of sin is death (Ro 6:23), consequently the deliverer from sin must pay that penalty in order to effect the redemption of mankind.

The apostle names the presentation (before the presence of the Father) of Christ's redeemed people as "holy and unblameable and unreprovable" (Col 1:22) as the ultimate objective of the reconciling work. This implies a gracious work done in them, answering to the gracious work done for them at the cross.

But before the goal is reached, a twofold human condition must be met; for the end is not to be dissociated from the process which leads up to it. So believers must "continue in the faith grounded [they have already been affixed to the rock Christ Jesus and are still there] and settled [firm in their convictions and loyalties]" (v. 23). Paul states the negative aspect of the same truth with the reminder that they are not to be "moved away from the hope of the gospel." This language is not a token of Paul's doubt as to the faithful continuance of his readers. In fact, the *if* ("provided," RSV) at the beginning, in the form it has in the original, implies rather than questions their fidelity. At the same time, with false teaching in the air, it was salutary to throw out a gentle warning against any shifting from the solid ground of the gospel.

The remainder of the verse seems at first sight an almost unnecessary addition to the thought. Surely the Colossians knew that the gospel they had received had been heralded in many other places besides their own city. But Paul deliberately makes his language extravagant in order to catch their attention—not only preached here and there, but "to every creature . . . under heaven." To be sure, this is hyperbole, for many places had not yet been reached, even those in the Mediterranean basin, to say nothing of regions beyond, whether in Europe or Africa or Asia to the east. We can better understand the apostle from what he wrote a few years before this to the effect that from Jerusalem to Illyricum he had fully preached the gospel (Ro 15:19). Actually he had visited only a few of the major cities. Yet the gospel had taken root and was spreading out from these centers into the surrounding country. And it was the imperishable gospel which was making this progress, not some perversion of it. The Colossians were not to get out of step with the rest of Christendom (see comments on 1:6)!

It is with subdued pride that the apostle adds the footnote that he has been made a minister of this good news. He was well aware of the superiority of this message to anything he had received from Judaism.

IN RELATION TO THE MINISTRY OF PAUL (1:24-29)

At the close of the preceding verse Paul described himself as a *minister*. The influence of that word carries over to what he now says about the suffering entailed in that service. Perhaps the *now* is intended to lay special emphasis on his present circumstances, the limitations imposed by his imprisonment. Refusing to complain or be depressed, he can only *rejoice,* knowing that his sufferings benefit the Colossians, as well as other believers. As his thought broadens out, he reflects that these sufferings

which affect his *flesh* are for the sake of the whole *body* of
Christ, the church.

But the way in which the apostle describes these sufferings is peculiar—as a filling up of what is lacking of "the
afflictions of Christ." One thing is certain, namely, that
Paul does not intend to suggest that the sufferings of Christ
in connection with His death need supplementing by any
one of his people or all of them put together. "The Colossians were the last to whom St. Paul would use, without
explanation, a phrase which would be so open to miscon-
ception, as tending to foster the delusion that either saints
or angels could add anything to Christ's work" commented
T. K. Abbott.[2] Paul's own statement in 2:14-15 would
contradict such an impression, in line with the totality of
teaching on the death of Christ in his letters. As a matter
of fact, the word *afflictions* is never used in connection with
the death of our Lord; so it must apply to His precross
suffering caused by the pressure of Satan and human ad-
versaries—not to speak of the apathy and unbelief of the
people. It is appointed to all believers to have a share in
this kind of suffering (Ac 14:22; Phil 1:29; 2 Ti 2:3). If
fellowship with Christ stops short of including participation in His sufferings (Phil 3:10), then the fellowship is
far from complete. Paul's desire is that the Colossians,
spurred by his sufferings, may themselves undertake a more
vigorous witness to Christ, cost what it may. This way of
ministering, with abandon, characterized the Saviour in
His earthly ministry. The servant is not greater than the
Master. In Paul this attitude and practice became a part
of his being, ingrained, as it were, to the very end of his
life (2 Ti 2:9-10).

Rather than dwell longer on the theme of suffering, the apostle repeats the statement made at the end of verse 23, that he had been "made a minister" (v. 25). And here, as a counterpart to the filling up of the necessary measure of afflictions, he cites the positive aspect of his task, the fulfilling of "the word of God." This he was pleased to do (Ro 15:16-17), and expected his colaborers to do the same (Col 4:17; 2 Ti 4:5). He was called to proclaim the gospel, so that everything else was secondary. Far from having planned this as a child or as a young man, Paul received this responsibility as a "dispensation [or commission] of God" at his conversion (Ac 9:15-16; 26:16-18). The same expression occurs also in 1 Corinthians 9:17. As a servant of Christ he was also a steward of the mysteries of God and must be prepared to render account to a Lord who demands faithfulness (1 Co 4:1-5).

To this greatest of all mysteries the apostle now turns (Col 1:26-27). It centers in Christ (cf. 1 Ti 3:16). Though the word *mystery* is used in more than one sense in the New Testament, the general idea conveyed by it is the divine purpose in salvation. This existed in the mind of God from all eternity. It remained largely hidden through the *ages* (epochs) and *generations* covered by Old Testament history, despite occasional prophetic foregleams. Then, in the fullness of time, it came to expression in the world through the coming of the Son of God. But the meaning and mission of Christ were not perceived by men. The wisdom of God behind the death of Christ was hidden from those who participated in it (1 Co 2:8). Naturally, then, ordinary men cannot be expected to understand or appreciate the consummation of this purpose and plan of

God in the age to come. But the saints can anticipate it, because Christ lives in them now as "the hope of glory" to come.

As used by Paul, the word *mystery* does not depend on pagan usage in connection with the mystery religions. Proof of this lies in the fact that whereas those religions enshrined their mystery or mysteries in cultic observances, the sacraments of the church are never labelled mysteries. To sum up, a mystery in the biblical sense relates to the divine purpose and can become known only by revelation, which limits it to those who respond to the divine disclosure of God's plan in the gospel message.

It was God's will to make known to His saints "the riches of the glory" of this mystery. Here the central idea seems to be that of the unexpected and unparalleled wealth of truth connected with the coming and presence of God manifest in the flesh (cf. Jn 1:14). Though that manifestation occurred in the context of Israel and in the land of Palestine, it was destined to be proclaimed and explained "among the Gentiles," for they were included in the purpose of God (cf. Ro 16:25-26). To make this more personal and precious to his readers, Paul defines it as "Christ in you, the hope of glory." The coming into the world and the crucifixion belonged to the first stage of the unfolding of the mystery; the resurrection and the ascension, together with Christ's residence *in* His saints, constitutes the second stage, which continues in force to this very hour; and the experience of being with Christ in glory will be the third and final stage. The *hope of* glory is Christ Himself, for His presence in His people gives substance to the promise of being glorified with Him at His coming again

(Col 3:4). This hope will never be dashed; there will be no disappointment (Ro 5:2-5).

With his unerring instinct for centralities, the apostle continues by saying, "whom we preach" (Col 1:28). He would not focus attention on the mystery or the hope but on Christ, who is the essence of both these spiritual realities. Here he departs from the pattern of reference to himself alone as a minister of the gospel (as in vv. 23-25) and includes others, perhaps to underline the truth that his companions and others were one with him in their proclamation and incidentally to hint that those who taught differently, especially at Colosse, were out of step.

But the preacher's task is not finished with the proclamation of the gospel. He must be prepared to take up the role of the pastor, to shepherd the sheep. The care of the saints involves "warning every man." As the apostle reviewed his Ephesian ministry in the hearing of the elders of that church, he included the reminder that for three years he ceased not to admonish (the same word is rendered "warning" in our passage) everyone night and day with tears (Ac 20:31). He saw the danger that the flock might be rent by wolves with their false doctrine and that forces from within might cause divisions. So if admonition and correction appear in the present letter, this is not to be thought of as strange. He is not singling them out, for this is part of his task as pastor-teacher. The more constructive aspect of his work is contained in the phrase, "teaching every man in all wisdom."

Emphasis falls heavily on *every man,* three times mentioned in this one verse. No one is without some measure of need, and no one is without the possibility of correction

and growth. It is possible that the errorists at Colosse were
seeking to appeal to the more intelligent and influential of
the Christian group, in the hope of making converts to
their viewpoint. In this case Paul's stress upon *every man*
is a reminder that Christianity is not exclusive in the sense
that it ignores some segments of the people in order to
cater to others. We know that the Gnostics were guilty of
this.

The goal of Paul as pastor-teacher is to "present every
man perfect in Christ Jesus." The word *perfect* has various
shades of meaning. In the absolute sense, it can apply to
God's character, meaning complete and without flaw (Mt
5:48). Paul sometimes uses it to denote the mature Christian in contrast to the babe in Christ (1 Co 2:6). There
may be some kinship with the thought of maturity in the
passage before us; but since the verb *present* looks to the
future, to the glorious day of Christ's appearing (as in Col
1:22), one can hardly avoid the conclusion that the apostle
has in mind that coming day when the limitations of the
sinful nature, that hobbles all believers in greater or lesser
degree, will be removed. Nevertheless, both the present
and the future seem to be present as contributing factors,
for even the babe in Christ will be made perfect at His
coming. What Paul desires is to reduce the gap between
spiritual immaturity and the ultimate perfection which
will dawn upon every child of God. He wants to prepare
the saints as fully as possible, so that their lives in this
present world will reflect to others a meaningful readiness
for that final transformation. Even the apostle knew that
he himself had not yet been made perfect in the absolute

sense (Phil 3:12), but he sought constant and increasing conformity to Christ.

What Paul has been saying about the shepherding and teaching of God's people applies in principle to all Christian workers (note the plurals in Col 1:28). But in keeping with the personal strain that appears in the passage (vv. 23-25), the apostle testifies to the intensity of his own commitment to this task (v. 29). In doing so, he uses two terms which demonstrate that he puts himself completely into his work. He *labors* ("toils," RSV) at his mission to the point of weariness and exhaustion, but keeps on. He regards it as a contest such as the athlete engages in, which demands all his powers in full exertion, *striving* (cf. 1 Ti 4:10 and 1 Co 9:24-27). The two figures of the worker and the athlete are brought together again in his admonition to Timothy (2 Ti 2:5-6).

Notable is the fact that Paul uses the present tense. Though he is a prisoner with all the limitations that imposes on him, yet he refuses to look on his work as terminated or even temporarily suspended. He continues to testify to his Saviour (Ac 28:20-31; Phile 10), to write letters, and to pray (1:3). The man whose persecuting zeal had been such that he had made havoc with the church has now turned all his energies into building up the faith which he once sought to destroy. But the secret of this unflagging endeavor is not merely his own determination; he is happy to acknowledge that Christ is at work in him *with power* ("mightily"). This divine potential is present in all believers (Phil 2:13), but not all appropriate it. Hence their labor is fitful and weak.

3

PAUL'S PASTORAL CONCERN
2:1-7

THE CHAPTER DIVISION disguises the fact that there is no abrupt change here, as the opening word *for* attests. We may say that the thought of the preceding verse is carried forward and particularized, since the root idea of *striving* is reproduced in the word *conflict* (which is better rendered "struggle" or "striving"). In this section Paul expresses his concern for the Colossians in much the same language that he has used in giving thanks and praying for them (1:3-14), a combination of satisfaction and solicitude.

Before tackling in earnest the doctrinal intrusion that needs exposure, the apostle wishes to establish as close a relationship as possible with his readers, so that they will not interpret his counsel as officiousness but that they will realize it grows out of a genuine desire to help them. Elsewhere he testifies that, in addition to personal burdens and trials, he had daily anxiety for all the churches (2 Co 11:28). Sometimes his striving for the saints was in terms of bearing persecution and providing therein an example of fortitude for believers (Phil 1:29-30). But in the present situation it is carried on within his own spirit as he wrestles in prayer for these brethren who are far away, and not for them alone but for those in nearby Laodicea. In both instances these people have not seen Paul, though they have heard of him and his labors through Epaphras and Philemon. Epaphras has been engaged in fierce spiritual warfare on behalf of these believers, wrestling in prayer for them (Col 4:12). Paul shares his soul travail. They were fellow servants not merely in name but in fact (1:7).

Having some knowledge of these believers through the help of Epaphras, what does Paul covet for them? He sets it forth in a series of statements, building one upon the other, and includes both the end to be realized and the human conditions that will make possible the realization (2: 2-3). He seeks for them encouragement in the inner man, that out of this individual fortifying they may find strength to develop a conscious unity among themselves, cemented by love, as the condition for understanding the mystery of God, even Christ, and the wealth of divine wisdom to be found in Him. The apostle is saying that the perception of God's truth is greatly affected by the state of human relationships within the body of Christ. Is it not significant that in writing to the Corinthians he put his great exposition of spiritual illumination (1 Co 1:18–2:16) squarely in the middle of his treatment of factions in the church? Perhaps the Colossians already were finding that tensions were mounting in their assembly, as some expressed interest in the new ideas that were being disseminated in their midst and others were resolutely and outspokenly opposed. Because human understanding is so limited, truth sometimes divides; but love always unites. In this case, however, it was error that was provoking division; so the preservation of unity should be easier than when fine

points of Christian doctrine are under discussion. Love
had the power to pull together hearts that were beginning
to be touched with coldness. With unity recaptured and
fostered by the Spirit, then the fruit of the Spirit, which is
love, would be free to point the way to richer understanding of the common heritage in Christ.

Paul desires for his readers *all* the riches of confident
understanding, answering to "all the treasures of wisdom
and knowledge" that are in Christ. Let not the word *mystery* frighten or discourage them. Granted that the treasures
are hid in Him, this does not mean that they are unavail-
able. He already has asserted that this mystery is now manifest (1:26). In the earlier passage, attention centered on
the fact that Gentiles were included, that Christ the hope
of glory was now resident in them. But here the focus is
on the riches of wisdom and knowledge contained in this
indwelling Son of God. The Christ, who in the days of His
flesh bade men not only come to Him but learn of Him
(Mt 11:28-29), is now immediately and intimately available. He is teacher and lesson, inexpressibly rich in both.
Paul is not saying here that God is Christ, as though to dis-
solve the person of the Father in the Son, but that the
mystery of God, which he wishes to impart, centers in
Christ. Men come to know God in His Son (Jn 1:18). To
this end our Lord kept making Himself known by word
and deed when on earth—not to call attention to Himself
in isolation from the Father but as one with Him and sent
by Him.

People marvelled at His wisdom (Mk 6:2), and He
Himself was aware of His uniqueness in this respect. The
queen of the south came to hear Solomon's wisdom, He

remarked, but a greater than Solomon was now there (Mt 12:42). Again, by His own confession, He had a knowledge of the Father that no man possessed; and He stood ready to reveal the Father to those who applied to Him (Mt 11:27). Now that He is glorified, surely His resources are no less than when He walked the earth. In fact, He *is* the wisdom of God (1 Co 1:24). The blessed Spirit has the responsibility to reveal the deep things of God (1 Co 2:10-11), to show to the servants of Christ the things of the Father and of the Son (Jn 16:14-15).

Over against the solid and lasting treasures to be found in Christ, Paul puts the "enticing words" and false reasonings of those who seek to take advantage of believers and turn them away from the simplicity of the gospel (Col 2:4). Both their manner and their matter are suspect. The Greek term rendered "enticing words" occurs nowhere else in the New Testament, but something of its flavor may be sensed from a papyrus document of the early centuries which describes the attempt of thieves to retain their booty by what we would call "fast talk." Evidently, Paul is suggesting that teaching contrary to the faith owes more to the skill and subtlety of its advocates than to any inherent truth in the doctrine that is presented. By contrast, those who proclaim the gospel rely on its truth and are content with a simple, sincere approach (1 Co 1:17; 2:1-5).

To this note of warning the apostle adds a word of commendation (Col 2:5). His pastoral experience, which included relationship with many congregations and individuals, had taught him the necessity of a balanced approach. A warm word of praise made the word of warning or rebuke much easier to accept. He wants his readers to

feel that, although he is far away in body and prevented
by circumstances from coming to them, he is with them *in
spirit*. He had written to the church at Corinth in a similar
vein, giving directions about dealing with a nasty discipli-
nary problem (1 Co 5:3-4). He was a factor to be considered, even though he could not be there in person. In
the present case discipline is not involved, only the assurance of Paul's sympathetic involvement with the readers
in their situation. It is not uncommon for two people who
have unusual rapport to experience definite impressions
concerning the other when they are separated. The writer
recalls that after a serious accident which befell him, he
received a letter from his closest friend, asking if anything
had gone wrong on a certain day at a certain hour. That
was the very time of the accident. By sheer desire and out-
going love, Paul had entered into the life situation of the
Colossians despite the fact that they were not known to
him personally. In his spirit he rejoices over them as his
imagination pictures them in their local setting. Worthy
of commendation is their *order* (see 1 Co 14:40), which
encourages him to think that they will not be swept off
their feet by persuasive talk or be inclined to depart from
the guidance which the present letter affords. In line with
their good order is the strength and stability of their *faith*
(cf. Col 1:23), which is the solid foundation on which all
Christian life and service must be built. And faith is not
some open-mouthed attitude of wavering gullibility, which
is ready to accept almost anything from almost anybody; it
rests firmly on *Christ*.

According to the foregoing passage (especially vv. 4-5),
doctrinal error has not yet succeeded in making significant

inroads into the congregation. The apostle hastens to add
what he hopes will furnish immunity against poisonous
teaching. He reminds them that they have already "received Christ Jesus the Lord" (v. 6). The importance of
the human messenger is not emphasized here, nor is the
manner of reception stressed, as though the apostle meant
to say that even as they received Christ by faith they are to
walk by faith (see Jn 1:12). That is true enough in itself,
but it is not the focus of attention here. The stress is on
the *fact* that they actually received the person of the Lord
as He was offered to them in the gospel, when the knowledge of the Saviour was faithfully transmitted to them. So
they have more than just a store of knowledge about Him,
for He Himself has been taken into their hearts.

But Paul counterbalances the historic, once-for-all reception with the necessity of continuing to *live* in Him—
to exercise their faith, so to speak, in terms of consistent,
obedient conduct. Christ is more than the object of faith.
He is the sphere in which Christian life must be lived out
to the glory of God.

The nature of the "walk" is now made explicit. *Rooted
in Christ* is a term that refers back to conversion, when they
received the Lord. God placed them in the soil that is ideal
for growth. Paul combines this agricultural figure with
one of construction—*built up in him*, as implied in 1 Corinthians 3:9. Both figures tell basically the same story:
progress and fruitfulness are the standards for Christian
living. A third consideration is to be continually *established* (or strengthened) *in the faith*. Whether Paul has
reference to the faith of his readers, as in Colossians 2:5, or
means the content of the things believed by Christians, as

in Jude 3, is uncertain. Either makes good sense. Perhaps
the word *taught* tips the balance slightly in favor of the second possibility. Paul is able to count on this: the Christ-
centered message of the gospel, with its implications for
Christian life, has been made known to his readers; and he
does not have to go back over the ground as though they
are ignorant. His task is rather to encourage and build up
and fortify the converts.

The apostle has one more admonition at this point. His
friends must not forget *thanksgiving*. A grateful Christian
is one who is not only informed and intelligent but also
satisfied in what he enjoys through his relationship to the
Saviour. As Paul had included thanksgiving in his praying
for his readers (Col 1:3), he urges this spiritual exercise
upon them also (cf. 1:12). A thankful spirit is good insurance against the temptation to depart in some way from the
faith.

4

WARNING AGAINST FALSE TEACHING

2:8-23

WHEREAS UP TO THIS POINT Paul has given hints that subversive activities were under way to draw the Colossians from the purity of the gospel and complete dependence on Christ (2:4) and has anticipated his positive answer to the theological aspect of the heresy in the marvelous passage about the preeminence of Christ (1:15-20), it is at this point in the letter that he begins the formal refutation.

THE DANGER (2:8)

Here the warning sounded in verse 4 is repeated, but in altered form and in stronger language. *Spoil* is more devastating than *beguile*. It sometimes has the force of kidnap and is a vivid picture of the determination to make converts which so often characterizes advocates of the various cults that operate on the fringe of Christianity.

In the situation before us, *philosophy* was the lure that was used. The ancient Greeks were famous for their philosophical systems, and during the Hellenistic age some Jews felt the attraction of these schools of thought and began to describe their own religion as philosophy. Although this is the only time the word occurs in the New Testament, the idea is present sometimes in Paul's use of *wisdom*, especially in the Corinthian correspondence. He chides the Corinthians with being wise in Christ (1 Co 4:10), as though they regarded the Christian faith as little more than one of the philosophies current in their land. It would be going beyond the evidence of our text to assert that Paul is lashing out at all philosophy as worthless or even dangerous. The kind he has in mind is clear from the further description of it as "vain deceit," a system which has no substance and no power to edify. Those who hold it are self-deceived. Why, then, should genuine believers in Christ leave the solid reality of the faith for a spiritual vacuum? As to its nature, it is based on "tradition of men" rather than on divine revelation. There is such a thing as Christian tradition, for prior to the writing of the New Testament the gospel and its implications for the lives of believers could only be communicated by word of mouth, in accordance with the authoritative teaching of the apostles. But the tradition in view here lies outside this sphere and could be classed with the traditions of the elders which Jesus rejected on the ground that they set aside the word of God (Mk 7:5-9). While in Jesus' day the traditions of the elders pertained to teachings developed over the years in Judaism about the proper application of the Mosaic law to life, in Colosse the tradition had to do with secret and speculative notions about man's relation to the universe and to God.

Not only is this philosophy geared to human tradition but to "the rudiments of the world," if indeed this is the correct translation. (RSV has "the elemental spirits of the universe.") There is considerable debate among scholars as to the first part of this phrase, which in the original is *stoicheia*. The term has an interesting history. It is closely related to *stoichos*, which means a row, and so comes to be used of the elements in a row and from this comes to mean the alphabet. Since the alphabet is the first thing in the learning of a language, the word comes to mean what is elementary (see Heb 5:12, "first principles"). It is also used for the elements of which the world is composed (2 Pe 3:10, 12). Finally, it is applied to the spirits which are thought of as controlling the forces of nature. Since the veneration of angels is referred to in Colossians 2:18 and since in verse 8 the *stoicheia* are contrasted with Christ, the possibility of a personal reference should be admitted; and the same may be said of the usage in Galatians 4:3. On the other hand, there are reasons for doubting that this is the correct appraisal of the matter. In pre-Christian Jewish writings, where angels are associated with physical phenomena, they are called *pneumata* rather than *stoicheia*. Furthermore, the use of *stoicheia* to designate elemental spirits has not been traced to a time as early as the first Christian century. It could be, of course, that Paul is using a term which the heretical teachers have employed, without committing himself as to the legitimacy of the concept involved; but in view of Paul's use of the phrase at an earlier time (in Galatians), this is not a probable solution. We know this much at least, that the teaching Paul refers to and is combatting was at fault because it did not conform to *Christ*. The implication is that by His redeeming work He cancelled whatever efficacy men imagined they could find in fleshly regulations designed to minister to the spiritual life. (See Col 2:20-23, where certain human precepts and doctrines are discussed.)

The mention of Christ starts the apostle on a lengthy statement (vv. 9-15) which resembles somewhat 1:15-22 in that both His person and work are recounted.

THE DEBT OWED TO CHRIST (2:9-15)

The apostle launches into a statement of the greatness of Christ. "In him dwells all the fulness of the Godhead bodily" (ASV). The Jews found it hard to think of God dwelling with men. At best the *shekinah* or glory cloud in the tabernacle and the temple was but a representation of His presence, a symbol of His nearness and availability. When Jesus of Nazareth claimed oneness with God (Jn 10:30) it created great offense. Of the risen, exalted Lord, Paul affirms that the Godhead dwells in Him and in such fullness that there can be no sharing or distribution of divine power and majesty to other beings, such as angels. This is the force of the word *all*. *Bodily* is hardly a reference to the incarnation as an event, since the apostle uses the present rather than the past tense in this sentence; though it certainly teaches that the incarnation continues to be a fact. It primarily reinforces the idea of concentration in one place as opposed to dilution through distribution.

A glorious truth follows immediately, almost too daring to put into words. "Complete in him" is his description of believers. This involves a play on words, since *complete* is the same root word in the original as *fulness*, which has just been used of Christ. There is no intention, of course,

of asserting deity for the saints, but rather it makes clear
that in the Saviour all the potential of the redeemed life
lies accessible and can be communicated, as faith draws
upon Him. It is helpful to compare Paul's statement with
statements in the prologue of John, where the Word is
pictured as becoming flesh and His inner glory made
known, full of grace and truth (Jn 1:14), followed by the
assertion that of His fullness we have all received, even
grace heaped upon grace (Jn 1:16; cf. Eph 3:19).

The structure of the sentence places emphasis on the
words *in him*, which prepare the way for the concluding
observation that He is the head of all rule and authority
(cf. Col 1:16). There is no need for believers to resort to
angelic intelligences for mediation or assistance of any
kind. Christ is sufficient for His people. The point already
has been made that He is the head of the entire creation,
as the one who brought all things into existence. Included
in this creation is the whole sphere of angelic beings. Consequently, if the same Lord is at once the head of creation
and the church, it is idle for Christians to look elsewhere
than to Him. As the apostle puts it, He is "head over all
things to the church" (Eph 1:22).

Lest the idea of completeness in Christ be considered
too vague, Paul begins to enlarge on it by explaining what
the Lord Jesus has done for His people in specific matters.
The mention of circumcision (Col 2:11) seems strange,
because the readers were Gentiles (1:27); but it does indicate a Jewish influence in the Colossian propaganda. It has
been suggested that the leaders may have insisted on it as
an induction rite into the mysteries of their system. If it
had been put forward as a condition for salvation, as in the

Galatian churches, the apostle would have dealt with it
here much more at length and with severity. The Jewish
idea of circumcision as symbolizing separation from Gentiles, who were regarded as unclean and degenerate, could
apply here, fitting the notion of superiority assumed by the
errorists. Outward circumcision had its place under the
old covenant (Gen 17:9-14), but even there it needed to be
accompanied by circumcision of heart (Jer 4:4). Circumcision "without hands" puts the new and spiritual in contrast with the old and physical. Under the new dispensation, believers in Christ are the true circumcision (Phil
3:3).

As to the significance of the term for the Christian, Paul
sums it up under the phrase, "the putting off of the body of
the flesh" (ASV). Since this is without hands, the flesh is
not corporeal here; rather it refers to the sinful nature of
man. The *body* carries out the desires of the flesh and so
becomes its instrument. By sharing in Christ's death, which
was a death to sin, the believer has been separated in principle from this bondage (cf. Ro 6:6). Clearly "the circumcision of Christ" does not look back to the rite as performed
on the body of the infant Jesus but is rather the circumcision which Christ provides to all who are in Him. Since
the text goes right on to speak of burial with Christ, the
circumcision of Christ must refer to the value of His death
for all those who are members of His body.

The ease with which Paul glides from circumcision to
baptism is not difficult to understand, since both are initia-
tory rites in connection with their respective covenants, the
old and the new. Back of the language of Colossians 2:12
we are to see the historic events of Christ's death, burial,

and resurrection, which constitute the core of the gospel message (1 Co 15:3-4). Here, as in Romans 6:4, these events are seen not as affecting our Lord in isolation but as involving all who belong to Him. The entry into baptismal waters and the following emergence serve as well as symbolic acts can to set forth the cleansing from the old life under the power of the sin nature and the embarking upon a new life lived in the power of God. Water baptism is not to be thought of in opposition to or in separation from Spirit baptism (Ac 2:38).

Lest any get the impression that the rite itself is able to effect this life change, the apostle is careful to add that, in submission to the rite, the candidate is expressing his *faith* in the God who raised His Son from the dead.

Whereas the Saviour was actually dead and then raised to life, sinners are *dead* by reason of their *sins*, unable to please God by responding to His will and not caring to respond. Such had been Paul's readers. Paul does not mean to say that they were spiritually dead because they were physically uncircumcised but only that their Gentile background conveyed a presumption of a sinful state even more grievous than would be expected in Jews, who had the light of Old Testament revelation.

The same power which wrought in Christ to raise Him from the dead has brought life out of death to these believers. They have been raised together with Christ. At this point (Col 2:14), Paul cannot refrain from including himself and all other Christians, for he himself had received forgiveness of sins and had experienced the joy of being set free from the burden and curse sins imposed. Spiritual life apart from forgiveness is simply inconceivable.

This matter of forgiveness of sins is so important that it
calls for a more extended treatment, given in verse 14. Our
sins are represented as an obligation to which we have
assented as one who sets his signature to a bond. (Cf. Phile
19, where Paul commits himself to pay to Philemon what
Onesimus owes.) This indebtedness stands menacingly
over against us as sinners, with its full documentation. It
has to do with *ordinances*, which according to Ephesians
2:15 relate to the commandments of the law. God required
obedience and we have not complied. In the failure of the
Jewish nation to keep the law, we are to read our own
condemnation as Gentiles. We failed in these representatives as dismally as we failed in Adam, and then we sealed
our guilt by personal transgressions. But the gospel imparts the good news that God in Christ took this bond
"out of the way" (set aside," RSV) so that the record no
longer stands against us. The damaging evidence has been
removed and forgotten. But the price of that removal can
never be forgotten, for it took the death of God's Son on
the cross to make us free. "Nailing it to his cross" is vivid
language to indicate how truly and fully Christ identified
with sinners, being made sin for us (2 Co 5:21). Onlookers
at the cross saw the superscription bearing His name and
the alleged charge against Him. Believers are invited to
see their sins nailed there, a debt nevermore to be assessed
against them.

The drama of the cross included unseen beings as well
(Col 2:15). Paul already has talked about "principalities
and powers" as created by Christ (1:16). Here he indicates the hostility of some of these powers and teaches that
the hour of apparent triumph for them actually meant

their humiliation and defeat. The language is too strong to interpret merely that angelic mediation of (good or neutral) angels was there set aside by the more powerful mediation of the Saviour. In his companion letter to the Ephesians, the apostle uses these two terms, *principalities* and *powers*, to describe the hosts of darkness against which the Christian must carry on spiritual warfare (6:12). They were not eliminated at the cross, but their ultimate doom was sealed. In fact, Christ made "a public example of them" (RSV), which every believing eye is able to see and appreciate, though these enemies of Christ remained hidden from sight. In the light of His triumph, these sinister forces need not be feared. They can be faced boldly and challenged in His name, at least by those who have been conquered by His love and are led by Him in triumph, as they make Him known to the world (2 Co 2:14).

THE DISTRACTIONS (2:16-19)

Here Paul exposes the groundlessness of certain external observances that were being insisted on at Colosse. Note the force of the *therefore*. If Christ has won a decisive victory at the cross, there is absolutely no need to be held in the grip of fear that failure to keep certain ordinances will bring disfavor and perhaps reprisals from angelic authorities. Nor is there need to be fearful of human criticism: "Let no man therefore judge you." Evidently such judgment was going on in the areas Paul indicates. Christians were being made to feel that, if they did not comply, they were not living up to their religious obligations. From the nature of the items which follow, it is clear that the pressure was coming from Jewish sources. The requirements

are legalistic. In dealing with similar matters in earlier
letters, Paul warned believers not to judge one another in
things which were really indifferent in themselves and
about which individual consciences, rather than external
authority, had to make the decision (1 Co 10:25-29; Ro
14:3-4, 13).

Here, however, he is not arbitrating between two groups
of Christians, the so-called strong and the weak, but is
warning the whole company of believers against needlessly
losing their freedom in Christ over such externals. Some
groups in current Judaism were more rigorous than others,
notably those who belonged to the Qumran community,
where an ascetic type of life was the rule.

Paul warns against being brought into bondage in matters of *eating* or *drinking*. John the Baptist had a restricted
diet because he was a Nazirite, but Jesus did not observe
such restrictions (Mt 11:18-19). Later on, at Ephesus,
similar propaganda was abroad, causing Paul to write
vigorously against it (1 Ti 4:1-5).

The word rendered "holyday" is *feast* (ASV) or *festival*
(RSV), referring to the Passover and the other annual
observances of the Jewish year. It is not Paul's purpose to
condemn all Christian interest in these festivals, since he
himself expressed eagerness to be present in Jerusalem for
Pentecost (Ac 20:16); and he could hardly avoid taking
part in the general celebration, even if his major interest
was the Christian significance of the day in view of the
advent of the Spirit (Ac 2:1). But for Gentile believers
to observe the Jewish festivals was unreasonable.

Included in this list is the observance of the *new moon*
festival, several times referred to in the Old Testament

(e.g., 1 Sa 20:18) ; but this is the only reference in the New Testament. Many peoples have observed this season as a time of joy for the reappearance of the light that rules the night. Apparently sacrifices were offered on that day in Israel (Num 28:11), and it was a time free from ordinary labor (Amos 8:5). Since the day had no specifically Christian significance, it naturally faded out of usage as the church became more and more Gentile in its composition.

The *Sabbath* is included in this list. The seventh day of the week was given to the Hebrews as the time of rest from work and journeying and the time for gathering in the synagogue to worship and to be instructed from the Scriptures. If the Sabbath were the day for Christian convocation, it could not have been treated as it is here, included with other items which were not binding on the believer. From the beginning of the life of the church, under the influence of the resurrection of Christ, the first day of the week was set aside for worship and remembering the Lord. As a matter of expediency Jewish believers, especially in Jerusalem, must have abstained from work on the Sabbath, so as not to offend their fellow countrymen. Since many of them would be required to work on the first day, it is probable that their own meetings were held late Saturday night after the close of the Sabbath and carried over into Sunday morning. This possibility is suggested by Luke's narrative of Paul's meeting with believers at Troas (Ac 20:7-11). Glancing back at the last three items in the text, it is noteworthy that they include observances of the year, the month, and the day (cf. Gal 4:10).

Now Paul evaluates all these things, calling them "a shadow of things to come" (Col 2:17). The same thing is said about the law in Hebrews 10:1, teaching us that the preparatory dispensation was simply a foreshadowing of the one to follow. Why go back to the old and its ordinances when the new has come? "The sketch is taken from the reality, and implies the existence of it. The shadow is the intended likeness of the substance. In other words, Christianity was not fashioned to resemble Judaism, but Judaism was fashioned to resemble Christianity. The antitype is not constructed to bear a likeness to the type, but the type is constructed to bear a likeness to the antitype. It is, in short, because of the antitype that the type exists. The Mosaic economy being a rude draft of Christianity, presupposed its future existence."[1] A good example of this truth is Paul's observation that Christ our Passover has been sacrificed for us (1 Co 5:7). In contrast to shadows, "the body is of Christ." There is no allusion here to Christ's physical body or to His body the church, for *body* is used in opposition to *shadow* and means substance or reality. Why should one grasp for a shadow when he holds the substance in his hand? The new age of the gospel has brought the blessings to which the old economy pointed. To return to the old is to turn back the clock and lose the blessed reality of the finished work of Christ with all its attendant mercies.

Colossians 2:18 is fraught with difficulties. The obscurities, which make it one of the hardest passages in the entire book to decipher, may be due in part to Paul's desire to show that he is familiar with what is being promoted at Colosse, which he does by crowding the text with terms that would be meaningful to his readers but which are obscure to us. It may be, too, that he is using language designed to show up the whole cult as ridiculous and thereby shame his readers into the realization of the folly of being taken in by it.

The RSV rendering runs as follows: "Let no one disqualify you, insisting on self-abasement and worship of angels, taking his stand on visions, puffed up without reason by his sensuous mind." The translation "disqualify" is based on the notion that the verb carries here the idea of acting as umpire and so depriving one of the prize he expected to receive. However, the idea of a prize often is not involved in the use of this word, so this aspect should not be pressed. Doubtless there is a close parallel to the warning against letting anyone judge (v. 16), that is, sit in judgment; only here the thought is intensified, so that something in the nature of a condemning judgment is in view.

"Insisting on self-abasement and worship of angels"—the main problem here resides in the first word, which ordinarily means willing or desiring. Aside from the question of meaning, however, is the matter of relationship in the sentence. In the original there is considerable awkwardness in taking it with the words that follow; but, if it be taken with what precedes and be rendered "wilfully," the meaning it has in 2 Peter 3:5 (ASV), then it serves to bring out the attitude of haughtiness and highhandedness that goes with the propaganda. This characterization is no doubt intended to expose the inconsistency of claiming to act in *self-abasement* (cf. Col 2:23, RSV). It is actually a false humility which asserts that one must not presume to approach the Most High directly and which insists that the path to the Almighty must be by the "worship of

angels," beings who are more exalted than man but inferior
to God.

"Taking his stand on visions"—this is quite different
from the KJV, "intruding into those things which he hath
not seen" (2:18). Our leading manuscripts omit the negative, so the idea is not of presumption but of something
experienced. What the visions consist of is not stated, but
Paul appears to be using the language of initiation into a
religious cult. The vision is a mark of the esoteric character of the religion, which the devotee must then try to
comprehend. "Taking his stand" may obscure the thought
somewhat, since the obligation expressed here is rather that
of going forward to the exploration of the mysteries seen
in the ecstatic state of devotion. Not only is all this unnecessary for the true believer, seeing that in Christ all
the treasures of wisdom and knowledge are his (2:3), but
also it is a grievous slight that must wound the heart of
the loving and all-sufficient Saviour. Paul minces no words
in showing how contrary to supposed self-abasement the
exponent of "the new way" really is, "puffed up without
reason by his sensuous mind" (v. 18, RSV). It is the attitude of superiority over the rank and file because of dab-
bling in things that they know nothing about. "The false
teachers claimed a higher intelligence, perhaps a deeper
spiritual insight, whereas the apostle declares that it was
carnal, not spiritual."[2]

So much for the exposure, but where lies the basic fault?
Just here, according to the apostle, namely, in "not holding
the Head" (v. 19). One can hold the doctrine of Christ
without firmly grasping Him as his very life, and there
must be life if there is to be growth. It is sad to see one

who has been numbered among the saints and apparently
a part of the fellowship become so enamored of speculation
and cultic "experience" as to make it apparent that he is
really spiritually dead. Christ is our life—as Paul is about
to say (3:4) —yes, Christ Himself and not some finely spun
theory that excites the imagination but ceases to draw upon
Him who is the very atmosphere of the redeemed soul.
Paul reminds his readers how the body, the church, is able
to grow. The life of the Head is pictured as causing the
increase in the body, which is a unit supported and held
together by the connections of the parts, as in the human
body (cf. Eph 4:16). Two ideas are combined: the har-
monious union and functioning of the various parts of the
body, and the growth achieved by the whole as the opera-
tion of God.

THE DELUSION OF SELF-DEPRIVATION (2:20-23)

Refutation of the heresy on the doctrinal side now has
been completed. There remains the necessity of disposing
of its tyranny over human lives in terms of ascetic prohibitions. Here the key is the death of Christ, not now in relation to sin but to worldly regulations imposed by those who
misunderstand the true nature of holiness. Death with
Christ, already considered in verse 12, is now set forth as
that which separates "from the rudiments of the world."
The redeemed are set free from man-made regulations
mistakenly designed to make one more holy. To accept
such restrictions is to admit that one is modeling his life
in terms of the world rather than of the new life in Christ.

The type of thought combated in Colossians is dualistic,
setting spirit and matter in sharp contrast. This means that

the body was regarded as essentially evil. What was to be done with it? Two opposite tendencies developed. One was to deny the body through ascetic practices, which seems to have been the earlier approach. Certainly it is the one found in this passage. The other was the opposite tendency, insisting that as long as the soul was kept pure, no amount of bodily indulgence could affect it. Such a viewpoint failed to appreciate the unity of man's being and was ruinous to morality. This latter position is stoutly resisted in 1 John 3:4-10 and other passages.

To avoid all misunderstanding, Paul proceeds to indicate the "ordinances" that are being insisted on, actually quoting them: "touch not; taste not; handle not" (Col 2:21). In view of the meaning of the original, the first and third should be reversed. This reveals the progression which makes the prohibition increasingly demanding. One must not handle or sample by tasting, and must even refrain from touching. By quoting in this way, the apostle is virtually mimicking the paternalistic instructions given by the false teachers to beginners in the cult.

The Mosaic code had restrictions concerning foods that were declared unclean. Those who accepted the vow of the Nazirite bound themselves to observe additional limitations, including abstinence from wine and avoiding contact with a corpse (Num 6). Those items involved taste and touch. These in Colossians may well be a combination of Jewish ordinances and the ascetic temper of early Gnostic thought. It is well known that the Qumran community went beyond the rest of their countrymen in demanding a well-regulated life, including simplicity of diet and clothing. This influence may have extended to Colosse, but it is not possible to trace this development historically.

Although *touch*, the first term in this series of three, is used of intimacy between the sexes (Gen 20:4; Pr 6:29; 1 Co 7:1), it is not likely that this is the meaning, for Paul hardly would have passed it by without discussion if that had been the case (cf. 1 Ti 4:3, where he resists prohibition of marriage). Furthermore, the present discussion relates to *things* that are perishable, which would hardly be applicable to marriage (Col 2:22).

The second prohibition, "taste not," implies fasting and is of great interest because of the possibility that it may have some connection with the visionary experiences noted in verse 18. It is common knowledge that those who received apocalyptic revelations frequently prepared for it by abstinence from food (e.g., Dan 10:2 ff.). But it is unlikely that in the Colossian heresy fasting was limited to preparing for visions. Fasting was practiced to some extent in the early church, particularly on solemn occasions or in crucial circumstances (Ac 13:2-3; 14:23); but it does not appear in the exhortations of the epistles. It was strictly a matter of individual choice or mutual agreement rather than something legislated. The emphasis in the New Testament falls rather on self-discipline as the key to dedicated usefulness in the kingdom of God (1 Co 9:24-27).

The freedom of the Christian, then, is one reason for resisting the imposition of human ordinances. But there is another, and Paul cites this immediately, pointing out that the prohibitions have to do with things that "perish

with the using" (Col 2:22). They are destined for corruption by the very act of consumption. More than that, these
ordinances are based on "the commandments and doctrines
of men." They lack divine authority. This observation
is couched in the language of Isaiah 29:13, which may be
the source of Paul's wording. It is perhaps more likely,
however, that he is consciously depending on our Lord's
use of that passage as reported in Mark 7:7. The Master
rebuffed the Pharisees and scribes for seeking to make
binding the traditions of the elders. Paul was aware of
much that Jesus said and did, despite the fact that he was
not His follower at that time. He even ascribed to Jesus
things that our gospels do not contain (Ac 20:35).

The concluding verse of this section is admittedly obscure and has received various interpretations. Since the
RSV is more lucid than the KJV, it will be followed here.
These human precepts do "have indeed an appearance of
wisdom in promoting rigor of devotion and self-abasement
and severity to the body"; and Paul is willing to concede
this, though with a touch of irony, as he piles one claim
upon another. The first item, *rigor of devotion*, is literally
"will-worship," hinting that it is not prescribed by God
but only by (the will of) man. Another possible rendering
is "self-made religion." *Self-abasement* in other settings
would be properly rendered "humility," but here it is only
a counterfeit of the real thing. *Severity to the body* need
not be associated only with fasting but could include denial
of sleep, of ordinary creature comforts, and possibly hints
at self-inflicted beatings—anything that would win the ac-
colade of "holy man" from other mortals.

If these are advantages (and Paul is conceding this only

from the standpoint of appearance), then what must be registered on the opposite side of the ledger? Such ascetic measures "are of no value in checking the indulgence of the flesh." Of special importance is the change from *body* to *flesh*. The latter refers to man's nature, including his spirit, outlook, motives, etc. Paul sees the real danger in asceticism as working injury to the inner man. If a man keeps his body in subjection and then gloats over his achievement, imagining that he has far outstripped the ordinary Christian, he has become the modern counterpart of the Pharisees, who loved to do more than the law required that they might take satisfaction in the fact that they were not as other men (Lk 18:11). Pride is one of the worst manifestations of the flesh; but asceticism goes further than subjection of the body, for it treats the body as an evil thing and thereby does despite to the natural order which God has ordained. The right course is to dedicate the body with all its powers to God for fruitful service (Ro 12:1).

5

APPEAL TO REALIZE POTENTIAL OF CHRISTIAN LIFE

3:1-17

ALTHOUGH THERE HAVE BEEN some commands and exhortations in the first two chapters, they have been predominantly warnings and remonstrances (Col 2:8, 16, 18, 20). An exception is 2:6-7, which remarkably prepares the way for the last two chapters where the practical implications of the gospel are spelled out for personal life and social responsibility.

ATTACHMENT TO CHRIST (3:1-4)

Although the watershed of the epistle has been reached, a hinge, *then*, binds what follows to what has gone before. Not without justice W. R. Nicholson entitles this paragraph "the true asceticism."[1] As pointed out in chapter 2, the false asceticism finds its fleshly gratification in its rigors toward the body; and this gratification, as an expression of pride and superiority, is just as reprehensible as the baser forms of physical indulgence. In the proper sense of the term, Christian life is the other-worldly life, for it finds in the contemplation of the celestial the inspiration and strength to manifest a transformed experience while still a part of the terrestrial scene. But this celestial outlook is no mere stargazing. It is the uplifting of the eyes of the heart to Christ, who has now returned to His heavenly home.

This preoccupation with "things which are above" is not born of wistfulness, as though one can find relief from the pressures of the world only by looking to a better world. It is not an effort to detach oneself, to find escape. Rather, it is the attitude found in Christ during the days of His flesh, who lived in the bosom of the Father even as He continued His strenuous labors among the children of men. The heavenly realm belongs to the saints; they have their citizenship there (Phil 3:20, ASV). Their resurrection with Christ, which Paul states as a fact rather than something clouded by uncertainty (cf. Col 2:12), would be meaningless if it did not involve participation in the heavenly, glorified life of the Saviour with ultimate union in the future, despite the present separation. But life in this world is not conducive to the maintenance of this heavenly tie, so that some resolution is needed—"seek those things which are above." Lest one stray into contemplation of glories not yet revealed, rivalling the false teachers in their visions, the apostle at once directs attention to Christ seated "on the right hand of God." His position attests His finished work (Heb 1:3) and proclaims His dignity and power (Ps 110:1-2; Phil 2:9-11). So the seeking of things above is not to be confused with aspiration after the so-called higher things of life idealistically considered, however legitimate they may be; but rather it points to the things that belong to resurrection life. Christians are not

immune to the pull of the temporal and material. They
need to be seeking all the time the things that belong to
the kingdom of God and His righteousness lest they be
caught up in worldly pursuits that rob them of spiritual
peace and power.

For the second time Paul mentions "things above," coupled this time with the injunction to center affection on
these things (Col 3:2). As someone has put it, "You must
not only seek heaven; you must also think heaven." But
again, it is not heaven as a place that is the real concern;
it is heaven as a spiritual reality which controls one's total
motivation. What is called for here is participation in the
mind of Christ. The "things on the earth" press upon us
daily, clamoring for our attention and participation; and
it is only one step to conformity, unless the renewal of the
mind restores perspective, reminding us that we are not
patrons of the world-system but pilgrims who have our
home elsewhere.

The reason for refusing response to earthly values lies
in the fact that we are *dead*. What is in view is our death
with Christ (cf. 2:20). It is not necessary to state that
there has been a resurrection also, since that has been declared sufficiently (3:1). What needs underscoring is the
truth that the life which was born out of resurrection with
Christ is not something independent of Him. "Your life
is hid with Christ in God" (v. 3). Anticipating this truth,
Jesus spoke to His disciples of the relationship they would
have after He left them—"ye shall know that I am in my
Father, and ye in me" (Jn 14:20). There is no thought of
maintaining that the hidden life means the believer is as
removed from the world scene as Christ is, which would

not be true. On the contrary, we are set here as lights in the world. The contrast involved is between the present situation, in which the source of our spiritual life is hidden from the world, and the future, when the relationship will be made manifest at His appearing. In the goodness of God many of the things which properly belong only to the consummation of salvation and to the life to come are made available to the saints in the present time. So it is that they partake of eternal life now, in Christ, not merely in the hereafter. If the psalmist could sing to the Lord, "All my springs are in thee" (Ps 87:7), how much more the one who has reposed his faith in the Son of God's love.

The story of the believer's relationship to Christ has a final chapter. It, too, is characterized by being *with him*, but then *in glory*. Moses and Elijah appeared with Christ on the mount in glory, but it was only a temporary experience. We shall be forever with the Lord (1 Th 4:17). When on earth Jesus gave to the disciples the glory which the Father had given Him, for they were now the representatives of the Father in the name of the Son. But He prayed that, when their work was done, they would be permitted to be with Him and behold His glory (Jn 17:24). The beholding will be only the prelude to sharing it (Ro 8:17), and this will involve the change to a glorified body (Phil 3:21). We shall be like Him at His appearing (1 Jn 3:2), fully conformed to the image of God's Son (Ro 8:29).

APPROPRIATION OF THE NEW MAN IN CHRIST (3:5-11)

This indeed is the point to which the thought is always moving in this section, but the old man and his deeds present a formidable obstacle which must first be dealt

with. Paul has established the cardinal fact that the believer, who has his place in the body of Christ, has been
involved in the great redemptive acts of the Saviour: His
death, resurrection, ascension and (in prospect) return.
Now the apostle selects out of this corpus of truth the one
item which is fundamental to the conquest of sin—namely,
death. In principle the sinful nature has been crucified
with the Lord, but there remains the necessity of acting on
that fact by refusing sin any right to continue its mastery
over the life that Christ has purchased by His precious
blood. *Mortify* simply means "put to death" (ASV) and
suggests the necessity as well as the possibility of dealing
decisively with the various sins that are mentioned, refusing them any claim to continuance. The command is a
call to take seriously the believer's death which has been
declared in verse 3. Christian morality is not an easygoing
thing that is satisfied with victory in one area while con-
fessing defeat in another, nor is it gratified with achievement now and then. It makes a radical demand upon the
disciple. If he is a new man, then he must demonstrate
that he is not the man he used to be. In an earlier letter
the apostle indicated a secret which greatly aids in reaching
this objective, namely, to reckon oneself to be dead to sin
(Ro 6:11). Sin is illogical, irrational, inconceivable for a
dead man. To bear this in mind when sin (which is far
from dead to us) seeks to allure us is a big help toward
achieving deliverance from its power.

Paul is not content to deal with sin in the abstract. He
is too practical for that. He knows that sin works through
the *members* of the physical body, even though sin has its
seat in the fleshly mind. So he says, "Put to death there-

fore what is earthly in you" (RSV). In his bodily existence
the child of God is still "upon the earth," where all sorts
of vices flourish. So, whereas he has a heavenly position
and inheritance, his walk is necessarily on the earth level
where temptation to sin lies in wait on every hand. *Fornication* and *uncleanness* involve directly the members of
the body, and these two terms are closely related. In the
Old Testament uncleanness is nearly always ceremonial in
nature, but in the New Testament it mainly denotes moral
impurity. This is the term Paul uses as a label for the
moral corruption of mankind that has resulted from giving
up the worship of God (Ro 1:24). Fornication was pre-
valent in the pagan world of Paul's day, presenting a grievous problem in the Gentile churches. In at least three
catalogs of sins the apostle put this first (1 Co 6:9-10; Gal
5:19-21; Eph 5:3-5). It was the great enemy of sanctifica-
tion (1 Th 4:3), about which all the Gentile churches
needed special warning from the Jerusalem council (Ac
15:29). It had taken a heavy toll, especially in Greek
civilization, as the lines of Matthew Arnold relate:

> On that hard pagan world disgust
> And secret loathing fell;
> Deep weariness and sated lust
> Made human life a hell.[2]

If the church could not offer a better way, it had little to
contribute to those who were concerned. Christian defection at this point hurt the cause of the gospel immeasurably
(1 Co 5).

Without changing the line of thought, the apostle moves
from outward acts to inward motivation as he adds to

things that must be put to death *inordinate affection* ("passion," ASV) and *evil concupiscence* ("evil desire," ASV). Not all desire is evil, but more often than not it tends in the wrong direction. Here the Christian ethic becomes penetrating. One cannot congratulate himself that he is free from sin if he manages to hold himself back from an overt act but at the same time finds the desire to commit the act remaining unchecked (cf. Mt 5:28). When Paul permits us a glimpse into his inner life, he tells us that conviction of sin came with the awareness that he could not meet the requirement of the tenth commandment (Ro 7:7, where "thou shalt not desire" is the literal translation). We all feel our helplessness at this point. If it is only by the Spirit that we can put to death the deeds of the body (Ro 8:13), how much more this is true of the desires of the mind!

Another sin that readily masters the human spirit is *covetousness*, against which Paul warns repeatedly (fifteen times in various forms in his writings). It has the thought of overreaching, of acting not only selfishly but arrogantly, not caring how much others are deprived or injured. Added to the damage done to others is the deteriorating effect on the character of the one who gives it free rein in his life. R. C. H. Lenski records the observation of a Catholic priest that during his long years of service all kinds of sins and crimes were confessed to him in the confessional but never the sin of covetousness.[3] It is indeed the unmentionable sin. *Idolatry* is the startling description the apostle adds to the word. A Christian is prone to recoil in amazement at this association, but it is simply drawing out the implication in our Lord's statement, "Ye cannot serve God and mammon" (Mt 6:24). *Mammon* is an Aramaic word meaning wealth or gain. Covetousness is an offense against man also. From the beginning the church felt the urge to share possessions with those of its number who lacked (Ac 4:32-37). Covetousness was bound to be regarded as an offense against *koinonia* (fellowship). In modern society where success is so often measured in terms of wealth, believers have the greater need to take seriously this warning against covetousness.

It remains for the apostle to set forth the divine reaction to these sins (Col 3:6). "The wrath of God" is the inevitable response (cf. Eph 5:6). Dare we imagine that even though God finds such things repugnant in the children of disobedience, He can look on them with complacency when they are present in the saints? The lesson is written large in the Old Testament, where repeatedly the God of covenant mercy found it necessary to chasten His people Israel when they fell into transgression. To act otherwise would mean unfaithfulness to His own righteous character. It goes without saying that when the Bible speaks of the wrath of God there is no thought of violent temper. Rather, His immeasurable displeasure with those who give themselves over to sin stems from His holy nature and is judicial rather than temperamental. According to Romans 1:18-32, God's wrath is even now at work, giving men up to sinful indulgence with all the consequences thereof, because they have given up Him. This does not by any means rule out His final verdict on the unrighteous when the day of wrath arrives and His judgment is made known (Ro 2:5).

Now and then it is a wholesome thing for the Christian to glance back at the pit from which he has been taken and

shudder a little before breaking out in gratitude to God
for His mercy. In line with this, Paul bids his readers
remember that their manner of life was at one time identi-
cal with that of the people who surround them in the pagan
world (Col 3:7; see also 1 Co 6:9-11 and Eph 2:2-3). They
hardly need to be reminded that it is the grace of God
which has made the difference.

Perchance the Colossians had lost just a little of the keen
edge of spirituality and had begun to be a bit lenient toward manifestations of sin that did not seem scandalous but
rather somewhat petty. If so, the apostle would bring them
up short by a ringing command paralleling the one given
in Colossians 3:5. "Put off all these" (v. 8). He is certainly including those sins mentioned already (v. 5) but feels
constrained to add to the list others which relate to the
temperament. Even with the addition of these items, the
sum total envisioned in "all these" is not reached, for they
comprehend, as one has said, "the universe of evil." All
that presently can be brought into view is a line of samples,
but they are enough to suggest the almost endless variety
of forms and shapes that sin can take.

The sins of temper and speech now come into prominence (v. 8). They need to be "put off" with the same
determination that must be used in dealing with the grosser
manifestations already noted. This command suggests that
the figure employed here is that of the removal of garments
(cf. vv. 9-10), not the dropping of something useful and
beautiful but the determined stripping away of the soiled
clothing that clings so closely, a true picture of the tenacity
of sin (cf. Heb 12:1, where "lay aside" is the same word
as in our passage).

Anger and *wrath* are not easy to distinguish, although the original terms permit some discrimination—the first being the deep-seated attitude; the other being violent eruption, the passionate outburst. Clearly the type of thing in view here is not the same as God's wrath (Col 3:6), which is not to be viewed as sinful since it is a manifestation of His righteousness. What must be put away is unwarranted indignation toward others. There is still room for the righteous variety, judging from the companion passage in Ephesians 4:26.

More fundamental than either of these terms, since it is the soil out of which they grow, is *malice*, or the disposition of animosity toward others that is ready to surface on the slightest provocation.

Such a spirit cannot readily refrain from asserting itself through the avenue of speech, so *blasphemy* must be included, in this case denoting slander of others rather than misuse of the divine name or wicked railing against the Almighty. Abusive speech is the idea, as in Romans 14:16 and 1 Corinthians 10:30.

Filthy communication means the use of foul language that grieves the one who hears it and defiles the one who speaks it. Surely this covers the retailing of off-color stories that may cause momentary merriment but leave a deposit of shame and reproach.

Lie not one to another (Col 3:9). To deceive a fellow believer or misrepresent something to him is an indication of lack of love. Moreover, it destroys confidence and interferes with the free flow of fellowship in the body of Christ.

Paul is concerned here not only with the inherent wrong in all the offenses he has mentioned but especially with the unreasonableness of their presence in the life of the Christian, who has "put off the old man with his deeds." The old and the new are incompatible. When was the old put off? Judging from Galatians 3:27, it was at baptism, for then the baptized put on Christ, as the apostle states. This in turn should be linked to Romans 6:6, where Paul explains that our "old man" was crucified with Christ. Baptism proclaims death with Christ to sin and resurrection with Him to walk in newness of life. Consequently, in the passage we are considering, the reminder is given that they "have put on the new man" (Col 3:10), fittingly symbolized by the fresh, clean clothing given to the baptized in place of their old garments. The radical nature of the change effected by identification with Christ is again and again put forward by the apostle, as in 2 Corinthians 5:17, "If any man be in Christ, he is a new creation: the old things have passed away; behold, new things have come."

Two observations are in order about the new nature ("man," Col 2:10). This is a provision, a definite gift from God. Yet it is also true that the new nature, when put on, has the capacity for growth, ever being *renewed*. In other words, the new birth or new creation is followed by the experience of progress and maturation, especially in *knowledge*. The new man in Christ is able to discern the will of God, and his great purpose in life should be to perform that will and so grow up into Christ (cf. Eph 4:15). From the use of *image* it is evident that the creation of man, as told in Genesis 1:26-27, lies in the background here. Elsewhere Paul contrasts the first and last Adam. (Ro 5:12-21; 1 Co 15:45-49), but here the new man in Christ holds the

center of attention. Yet, the Genesis account is reflected
not alone in the use of the word *image* but also in the
double significance of the word *man*. In Genesis man is
both the individual (Adam) and the race (mankind).
Adam *was* the race to begin with. Similarly, the new man
in Christ is not only the individual believer but in the
corporate sense includes all who make up the body of
Christ, to which Paul immediately directs attention (v. 11).

The connection of thought with the preceding statements is probably to be found in the injunction to "put
off" (v. 9), even though it is not repeated here. Just as
that command is based on the spiritual truth that the Christian, as the new man, has put off the old and now needs to
act that way, so the saints who make up the new man in
the corporate sense should realize that they must do their
part to ignore the distinctions which time and circumstance
have built up, distinctions which lose their significance in
the body of Christ save as a reminder of the unifying power
of the gospel of the Lord Jesus. God has obliterated these
worldly distinctions, so it is wrong to carry them over into
Christian relationships.

Alexander the Great had tried valiantly to bridge the
gap between Greek and Oriental civilizations. When the
Romans in turn took over the Near East and became the
caretakers of the fragmented empire of Alexander, they
tried to break down the national, racial, and cultural bar-
riers that divided their subjects. But their success was
limited because their approach was too superficial. "As a
kingdom of this world . . . the Roman Empire could not
create the unity achieved through the gospel. It stood for
devotion to a code, not to a Person," commented W. Fair-

weather.[4] The distinctions named here may need to be retained for the sake of identification (Ac 22:3; cf. 1 Co 9:19-22), but they do not interfere with the spiritual oneness bestowed on all who belong to the body of Christ.

The wording of the passage, "where there is neither Greek nor Jew," is unfortunate, for it suggests that these two great divisions of mankind are excluded from participation in the church, which is foreign to the thought. The original is plain: *where there is not Greek and Jew;* that is, the distinction, the tension, is no longer there. Notable is the fact that Paul says nothing about Romans. Not once does he mention them in any of his epistles. But they are included here in the term *Greek,* which is used as a synonym for *Gentile* (cf. Ro 1:13-16).

A second distinction, "circumcision nor uncircumcision," is ruled out. It has been seen already that there was pressure on the Colossian believers to accept Jewish regulations as appropriate to their lives (Col 2:16). Furthermore, Paul's allusion to circumcision as adequately accomplished in Christ (2:11) is a reminder of Judaizing propaganda which required resistance among the saints. The apostle's teaching on circumcision and uncircumcision in 1 Corinthians 7:17-19 should be consulted for its bearing on the present passage.

Passing from religion to culture as the basis for distinction, the apostle mentions *barbarian* and *Scythian,* both of them in implied contrast with Greek. Barbarians included all who were not participants in Graeco-Roman civilization; and of these the most despised were the Scythians, infamous for their cruelty and injustice. In the seventh century B.C. they invaded Palestine and left a memorial in the

Greek name for the city of Beth-shean, namely, Scythopolis (city of Scythians). Certain passages in Jeremiah (1:13-15; 4:6; 5:15; 6:1) warning of a dreadful invasion from the north may refer to the Scythian army. In his *Dialogue with Trypho,* Justin Martyr mentions that even a Scythian can be saved.[5] This was regarded as a blot on Christianity by enemies of the faith, such as Celsus; but believers gloried in this truth.

A further division involves *bond* (slave) and *free.* Since Paul wrote his letter to Philemon at this same time in which he reminded his friend that the slave Onesimus was to be regarded as his brother in Christ, it was appropriate to include this item, since Philemon was a member of the Colossian church. Assuming that this Christian gentleman acted on Paul's request by receiving Onesimus in a kindly, forgiving spirit, the church would have a vivid illustration that this social barrier was dissolved by the power of Christian fellowship.

But the key to unity is not in believers, except in a derived sense. It lies in Christ, who is their common Lord. He is the acme of importance (*all*) and the interpenetrating presence in which the highest type of unity is achieved (*in all*).

APPLICATION OF CHRISTIAN PRINCIPLES (3:12-17)

Here, as in the previous section, the language of clothing is used to convey the teaching. This has apparently determined the order of statement, since exchange of garments demands that one be put off before another can be put on. Having disposed of the old, it is now in order for the believer to accept the new. However, the matter of sequence

hardly can be pressed, for both Scripture and experience
teach that the most effective way to deal with the sins that
stubbornly cling to their victims is to clothe oneself with
Christ in all His transforming power (Ro 12:21; 13:14).
This is the truth strongly put forward in Thomas Chalmers'
famous sermon, *The Expulsive Power of a New Affection.*[6]
Leaves that successfully cling to a tree throughout the win-
ter, defying rain and wind and frost, are forced off when
spring brings the flow of sap to bear upon them. The new
supplants the old.

Having regard to Paul's *therefore* (Col 3:12) we are
able to locate the connection of thought in his previous
statement that believers "have put on the new [nature]"
(v. 10). What is true in principle must be made true in
practice. So the characteristics of the new nature are now
spelled out. "Bowels of mercies," though fairly literal,
does not convey the idea as well as *compassion.* Ancient
writers have included under the term rendered "bowels"
several organs—stomach, heart, spleen, liver, lungs, and
kidneys. It was likely their softness which prompted the
metaphorical application (cf. the popular expression, "have
a heart"). Bearing in mind that the new man has reality
only in Christ (3:3), it is legitimate to explore the possibility that the features detailed in this verse are simply so
many facets of the character of the Lord Himself. Again
and again the gospel writers relate that the miracles of
Jesus were prompted by a need that touched the marrow of
His compassion (Mk 1:41; Mt 9:36). Surely the Saviour
does not change His character when He takes up His abode
in His people (Heb 13:8). He is still the epitome of *kind-
ness* (cf. 1 Pe 2:3, where *gracious* comes from the same

Greek root). *Humbleness of mind* belongs to Christ, according to His own testimony; and the same applies to *meekness* (Mt 11:29). Paul acknowledges the *longsuffering* of the Lord Jesus in his own life as he looks back on his career as the persecutor of the church and thereby of the Lord Himself (1 Ti 1:16). Understandably, several of these terms appear also in the listing of the fruit of the Spirit (Gal 5:22-23), since by the Spirit Christ abides and comes to fullness in the saints.

Closely allied to longsuffering is the attitude of "forbearing one another" (Col 3:13), which involves an element of leniency, a willingness to suspend a rightful demand out of consideration for the plight or weakness of a fellow believer. It finds its supreme example in God Himself (Ro 2:4; 3:25). "Forgiving one another" is even more far-reaching, for it cancels the wrong or the obligation. Here the divine example is stated as in Ephesians 4:32, with the difference that in the Ephesians passage forgiveness is rooted in God and extended for the sake of Christ, whereas here the Lord Jesus appears as the author of forgiveness in line with the Christo-centric emphasis of Colossians. The Lord's Prayer contains a petition touching forgiveness, where the divine and human action in forgiveness are linked (Mt 6:12). It is a mistake to construe this as legalistic on the ground that forgiveness from God is dependent on prior forgiveness of one's fellows. We are not forgiven by God *because* we forgive one another or simply *to the degree* that we forgive one another. God is the initiator of forgiveness and what He bestows is not to be measured by the extent to which we have extended our forgiveness to others. However, it is futile to seek forgiveness from

God if one has an unforgiving spirit toward another person.
For God to extend forgiveness under those conditions
would only encourage the perpetuation of that very spirit,
and God would become a party to the wrong.

Retaining the thought of clothing introduced in Colossians 3:12, the apostle gives to *love* ("charity") the place
of honor as that which binds the other virtues together and
in so doing imparts to all the elements of Christian character its own peculiar nature, its power to unite and to perfect (v. 14). If this is the correct understanding of the
thought, then the rendering *"above* all these things," while
it safeguards the preeminence of love, is a poorer rendering
than *"over* all these things." Since the new man is the creation of God, made in His image (v. 10), and God is love,
this virtue is imperatively needed as the bond of fellowship
in the body of Christ. Our Lord Himself recognized that
the realization of unity among His followers depended upon the divine love freely operating in them (Jn 17:23, 26).

Peace works hand in hand with love to maintain this unity. According to our leading manuscripts it is "the peace of
Christ" (Col 3:15, ASV) concerning which Paul writes,
the peace that the Saviour gives to His own (Jn 14:27).
The thought does not express but rather builds upon the
basic truth of reconciliation to God. Only souls at peace
with God can be at peace with men. Doubtless it is this
aspect that is in view when Paul insists that this peace must
"rule in your hearts." But by adding the reminder that believers are called to peace "in one body," the ultimate appeal is to maintain the unity of the saints in that body
(Eph 4:3). It glances back, no doubt, to the sins that

imperil the welfare of the Christian community life, such sins as the apostle has warned against in Colossians 3:8 and 9. It would be ironical if Christ our peace, having effected harmony between Jew and Gentile (Eph 2:14), should then have to behold His body disturbed and, as it were, dismembered because His own people refuse to let His peace arbitrate and rule. The appeal to be *thankful* fits in well at this point, for the thankful Christian is easier to get along with than one who is always complaining. A grateful spirit promotes unity by encouraging others to emulate it.

Paralleling the peace of Christ is "the word of Christ" (Col 3:16). It must likewise have a determining influence in the church as the common possession of the saints. Although the word of Christ could mean the message about Christ (the gospel), it is more likely to mean in this setting, where teaching is emphasized, the word which Christ spoke. Believers did not yet have the New Testament to refer to, but they received knowledge of Christ's teaching from the tradition that was handed down from those who were with Him (Lk 1:2). Through His apostles and others, Christ continued to teach; for it was His word that they declared. (This is the implication in Ac 1:1.) Despite the fact that Paul seldom quotes any saying of the Master, his magnifying of the word of Christ clearly shows that he was far from ignoring the content of what Jesus taught. There is a kinship between *dwell* and Jesus' own requirement that His words should *abide* in His disciples (Jn 15:7). If the word of Christ is to dwell *richly*, it has to be cordially received, mixed with faith, appropriated in its fullness, and translated into action. If it is shared unselfishly in the group, no life remains spiritually poverty-stricken. This seems to be the force of "in you," namely, as a company of believers.

It is probable that "in all wisdom" should be taken with what follows, describing how the word of Christ is to be used in teaching rather than as indicating the manner of its dwelling in the saints. The phrase already has been used by the apostle in his prayer for the readers (Col 1:9). What is very clear is the necessity of having the word deeply planted in the heart before one can think of "teaching and admonishing one another." *Teaching* points to positive instruction calculated to build one up in the faith; *admonishing* relates to the corrective function of the truth (see 2 Ti 3:16). The church of Colosse did not have an apostle in its midst; and even its founder, Epaphras, was not available to help them. But they had the Spirit of truth, and He indwelled each one of them. Instructing *one another* implies a mutual responsibility. All the saints have a work of ministry, and this includes teaching (Eph 4:12). That this is not simply theory may be seen from the picture Paul gives of believers gathered for a public service at Corinth. Each one, he tells us, had a contribution of some kind to make, with edification the common goal (1 Co 14:26). Tucked away in this passage is the purpose of prophesying, namely, that all may learn and all be encouraged (v. 31).

This passage from 1 Corinthians is valuable also since it agrees with the verse before us in giving some prominence to the usefulness of *singing* as a means of edification for the church (1 Co 14:15, 26). But the problem in the Colossians passage is that the teaching and admonishing seem to be tied right in with the use of "psalms and hymns and spiritual songs." It is particularly hard to see how admonition would be conveyed through these channels, which are more naturally thought of as involving praise. Probably we are to understand that a separate activity is in view here—singing as distinct from teaching, with both activities springing out of the possession of the word of Christ in the heart. The RSV rendering is as follows: "Let the word of Christ dwell in you richly, as you teach and admonish one another in all wisdom, and as you sing psalms and hymns and spiritual songs with thankfulness in your hearts to God."

Students of Colossians have often commented on the almost complete lack of mention of the Holy Spirit in this book and have thought it strange. (1:8 is the sole place of occurrence.) But it should not be overlooked that there are two passages in which the word *spiritual* occurs (1:9; 3:16). "Spiritual songs" are probably those which are inspired by the Spirit (cf. 1 Co 14:15). While the early church used the psalms of the Old Testament and hymns of praise, there is good reason for thinking that new compositions were framed under the inspiration of the Spirit to include the newer elements of truth that had not been revealed under the old covenant. The psalms, for all their richness, do not suffice for a Christian hymnology.

To sing is good, but to sing "with grace" in the heart is better. The reference to the heart rules out any possibility that the apostle is using the word *grace* in the classical sense of gracefulness, as though the singing must be finished artistry. Grace could have its usual force here, in which case the heart is moved to sing in response to all that God has done in His lovingkindness. This grace is greater than circumstance, enabling men to sing when suffering pain or indignity, as Paul and Silas did at Philippi (Ac 16:25). Occasionally the Greek word, translated *grace* here, has a specialized meaning, which also fits well here: it can mean thankfulness (see 2 Ti 1:3, "thanks"). This would involve a heavy concentration on this theme (see Col 3:15, 17); but it is not impossible, since the point may well be that the same attitude which is encouraged in the specialized area of singing is then extended to include everything a believer does. Incidentally, *to sing in the heart* does not mean that the singing is unexpressed, but only that it is heartfelt.

At this point Paul does a characteristic thing, moving from the specific area of singing out into the wide arena of life in general, reminding us that the attitude of thankfulness is to accompany all we do (v. 17). Another example is found in 1 Corinthians 10:31 where instructions regarding properly safeguarded eating and drinking are extended to include all that one does—everything must be in terms of God's glory. The combination of *word* and *deed* as comprehending the whole of outward life in relation to others is fairly common. These are the two terms often used to gather up the aspects of our Lord's ministry on earth. Paul applies them to believers not only here but in 2 Thessalonians 2:17. What is especially noteworthy about the passage before us is the clear implication that doing is not simply a matter of acting but includes speaking. In His public teaching Jesus underscored the same truth, indicating that men would be held accountable for their words, even for those carelessly spoken (Mt 12:36-37). The truth is that both speaking and acting are revelations of the inward man.

The guiding principle for right action, whether by word or deed, is to "do all in the name of the Lord Jesus." This does not mean that His name should be invoked in connection with all that is said or done, which would be a highly mechanical procedure, but rather that in everything the believer should act as one who bears the divine name and has a responsibility to act in a way that will not bring reproach on that name. The privilege and power of the use of the name is balanced by accountability for honoring the person of Christ, who has graciously identified Himself with His own.

"Giving thanks" is one way in which the acknowledgment can be made of the great blessing enjoyed by the one who has Christ in his heart, and with Him all divine resources.

6

HOUSEHOLD OBLIGATIONS

3:18—4:1

SINCE THE FAMILY is the basic unit of society, the application of the gospel in this realm is bound to make Christianity a powerful force in the community. By its stability, the family is a means of evangelizing those who are impressed by daily examples of gentleness, love, and sobriety. The gamut of relationships within the household is included in this passage, not omitting even those who are slaves. One might think that Paul could be excused from mentioning such matters in a letter designed to deal with a special problem at Colosse. The very fact that he nevertheless has so much to say on the domestic front heavily underscores the realization of church leaders that the reputation of the gospel often was made or broken here. In view of the insistence of false teachers on asceticism, it was doubly important to magnify the institution which would be especially endangered by such a doctrine.

WIVES TO HUSBANDS (3:18)

Not only here, but in Ephesians 5:22 and 1 Peter 3:1, wives are addressed before any word is given to the husbands. This may point to the fact that the teaching then current in the church on this matter had become standardized, so that the language used and the order in which items were taken up were now fairly fixed. If we inquire as to why the wives should head the list, a possible answer is that the wife is the key figure in the home. Her relationship to the husband on the one hand and to the children on the other is pivotal. Notable is the fact that the wife is not called on to love the husband, which is taken for granted. Rather, the injunction is to *submit* to the husband, not merely in the conjugal sense (1 Co 7:3-4) but as the proper stance in recognizing the headship of the husband over the home. A woman who is not prepared to proceed on this principle is a poor candidate for marriage. Feminine objection to the idea of submission, however reasonable it can be made to appear in the light of current societal attitudes, loses its force in the face of Christ's submission to the Father (1 Co 11:3). In no way can we imagine that the Saviour counted it a reproach to take this place of subordination. It was taken voluntarily, with the realization that essential equality with the Father was not affected (Jn 10:30; cf. 1 Co 11:11). The apostle reminds the wives that this submission "is fitting in the Lord," meaning "befits Christian women." This expression, which Paul uses some forty times, emphasizes the Christian obligation in relationships and has a different force from *in Christ,* which speaks of our basic position in relation to God (2 Co 2:17).

HUSBANDS TO WIVES (3:19)

Now it is the husbands' turn. They are charged to *love* their wives (Col 3:19). To be sure, all believers are admonished to love one another; but the love of a husband for his wife has a special character, ideally modeled on that of Christ for His church, which means that it is much more than a sentiment. To measure up, it must be sacrificial (Eph 5:25). Love, then, is a duty as well as a privilege. It need not lose its spontaneity because it is commanded. The command simply underscores its importance. "Be not bitter against them": "It is useless to call your wife 'honey' if you act like vinegar toward her," quipped A. T. Robertson.[1]

CHILDREN TO PARENTS (3:20)

The fruit of marriage is children, and there is a word for them (Col 3:20). Observe that they are directly addressed; their obligation is not committed to the parents to be passed on to them. They are treated as responsible to God as well as to their parents. Incidentally, the direct address presupposes that they will be in church as this letter is read to the congregation. Paul was accustomed to their presence in the groups to which he ministered. *Obey* is the key word here; and the loopholes are plugged, for the command covers "all things." It is easy to obey parents when the thing required is agreeable to one's own desire or when it is convenient. But partial obedience is no true obedience, for it leaves a margin for one's own will to operate. What if Jesus Christ, as the Son of the Father, had obeyed in all things except the cross! Unquestioning obedience is lifted above the level of merely human relationship. It is "well pleasing unto the Lord." A child may well wonder if his position, one of immaturity and dependence, provides any opportunity to please the Lord. The apostle's answer is that not a day goes by without such opportunities in the home. Obedience to parents is the steppingstone to obedience to God.

FATHERS TO CHILDREN (3:21)

The command to the children could leave them glum, feeling imprisoned by parental authority. But Paul has not finished. There is another side to the coin. Fathers are warned not to *provoke* (irritate) their offspring, which can happen if the requirements laid down are petty or unreasonable or reiterated so as to amount to nagging. Happy is the home where a single word of command is accepted as adequate and is acted on without delay. A discouraged, dispirited child may go through the motions of obedience; but resentment is building up within him, well calculated to produce trouble in years to come.

SLAVES TO MASTERS (3:22-25)

In the comprehensive sense, the household in the first century included the slaves as well as members of the family proper. (The reference to Caesar's household in Philippians 4:22 doubtless had slaves chiefly in view.) Paul's allusion to them would have special interest to the church at Colosse because of Onesimus, who was sent back to Philemon at the same time this epistle reached the church. Observe that the letter to Philemon is addressed to the church in Philemon's house, which means that this brother could not deal with his runaway slave in a manner contrary to Paul's pleas, without risking the displeasure of his fellow Christians. This does not mean that Paul wished to embarrass him. Rather, he knew his man well enough to know how he would act, in full agreement with the apostle's request.

Christian slaves (Paul is writing only to such rather than to slaves in general) had a double obligation. One was obedience to their earthly masters. Here the temptation was to render "eyeservice" (Col 3:22), that is, to be solicitous to comply with the master's wishes when he was observing, so as to make an impression of fidelity and industry. One who would do this would almost certainly be prone to slacken off and become dilatory when the master was not looking. It is by attending to the other admonition of the apostle that the slave can avoid such an "in-and-out" performance, namely, by "fearing the Lord" (ASV). This will have the effect of giving him "singleness of heart," which is set over against eyeservice and indicates straightforward motivation behind one's actions. Bond service to a master will be of a higher order if rendered as unto the Lord. Whatever the job, whether arduous or light, whether distasteful or pleasant, it can be carried out cheerfully and "heartily" (v. 23) as long as the believing slave sees beyond the earthly master to the Master in heaven whom he must please first of all.

As an encouragement to this kind of service the apostle adds the observation that it will bring "the reward of the inheritance" (v. 24) from the Lord. This promise must be viewed in light of the fact that a slave had no legal right to an inheritance on earth even if one should be left to him. Normally he was not given wages. (Sometimes a kind master would set aside wages in order to accumulate a fund by which the slave could purchase his freedom.) His position was entirely different from that of the son and heir

(Gal 4:1-7). But the Christian slave could look forward
to being treated on the same basis as the free man, when he
stands before the Lord to receive his reward for faithfulness
and goes on to reign with Him.

By contrast, the unfaithful slave has only the prospect of
suitable recompense from the Lord for the *wrong* that he
commits against his master. Here the apostle uses the same
word that he employs in describing what Onesimus may
have done to Philemon, for which forgiveness is now sought
(Phile 18). Some have thought that in verse 25 Paul is
speaking of masters who have mistreated slaves and will be
judged for it. But A. S. Peake pointed out that "it is in-
credible that Paul should console the slave or encourage
him in his duty by the thought that for every wrong he received, his master would have to suffer."[2] It is only in the
next verse that the masters come directly into view. The
suggestion of F. W. Beare is helpful, namely, that the
lenient treatment recommended by Paul for Onesimus was
seen by the apostle as containing an element of danger.
Other slaves might feel they could commit wrongful, in-
jurious acts against their masters and make a similar break
for freedom. Paul warns against the assumption that Christian slaves can act as Onesimus (who was not a believer at
the time of his offense) did and escape a reckoning with
God. There will not be any favoritism shown just because
they are slaves and for this reason objects of pity.[3]

MASTERS TO SLAVES (4:1)

"Servants" is the KJV wording, but this could give a
wrong impression, as though hired servants were in view.
Beyond question the verse has to do with slaves, as is sug-

gested by the contrast with "masters." The latter are en-
joined to provide "just and equal" treatment for their
slaves. However, the Greek word for *equal* also means fair,
which is the more likely meaning here. While the slave
had equality in the spiritual sense (3:11), he did not have
it economically or socially; otherwise he would no longer
be a slave. Paul does not follow up his injunction by the
observation that slave and master are one in Christ, but
by a gentle reminder that the master must give account for
his treatment of slaves to "a Master in heaven." Or does
he mean, "Let the great Master's treatment of you be the
model of your treatment of them"?[4]

Christianity did not campaign to abolish slavery. The
time was not ripe for that. But it did seek for a betterment
of relations between bondsmen and their masters. Paul's
words must be read in the light of the conditions of the
time. Slaves were property. Masters had complete control
over them, even to putting them to death on the slightest
provocation. Cruel treatment inevitably produced resentment, which sometimes resulted in acts of revenge. That
the requirement laid down by Paul in this passage is min-
imal may be seen from his letter to Philemon, in which he
pleads for love and forgiveness toward Onesimus and even
hints at the possibility of making him a freedman.

7

CONCLUSION OF THE EPISTLE

4:2-18

APPEAL FOR PRAYER (4:2-4)

THE APOSTLE approaches this subject by giving at the outset some general directions. First, he urges his readers to *"continue* in prayer" (Col 4:2; see Ro 12:12). This is similar to his appeal elsewhere to pray without ceasing (1 Th 5:17). For this kind of attention to prayer one can find illustrations in the life of the early church: the apostles prior to Pentecost (Ac 1:14), the converts who responded to Peter's preaching (Ac 2:42), and the apostles once more (Ac 6:4). Second, prayer calls for *watchfulness,* which is the necessary condition of the believer if steadfast continuance is to be realized. The word means to be vigilant, wide awake, alert. It is what our Lord requested of the disciples in the garden (Mt 26:38, 40, 41). Third, *thanksgiving* is named as the proper spirit in which prayer is to be made (Phil 4:6). Thanksgiving is almost as much a hallmark of Colossians as is joy for Philippians.

Having touched on the matter of how to pray, the apostle now pleads for prayer on behalf of his companions and especially for himself in view of his circumstances as a

prisoner (Col 4:3-4). That he does not wish to claim all
the attention of his readers for his own situation is evident
from the *also*. In other words, "Granted that you will
doubtless have much to pray about, do not forget to include
us." The apostle may be thinking of Timothy (1:1) and
possibly of Epaphras and others who are named toward the
end of this closing chapter.

But he is especially concerned with his own need, as he
goes on to explain. It is not a personal need, such as his
health or mental attitude toward his imprisonment; but
his desire is that, despite his restrictions, he may have opportunity for the declaration of the gospel. That he had
government permission to preach is clear from Acts 28:30-
31, but that did not necessarily insure that he would always have people to whom he could witness. Elsewhere
Paul uses the word *door* to indicate an opening for testimony (1 Co 16:9; 2 Co 2:12). God must provide the
opportunity, hence the need for intercession by the saints.
"A door of utterance" (Col 4:3) is not the ideal translation,
since it fails to take account of the definite article. "A door
for the word" is what Paul seeks, making the thought
slightly different from the request in Ephesians 6:19, where
"utterance" is the correct rendering.

The apostle goes on to define the word as "the mystery of
Christ" and says that on account of this he is in bonds, a
prisoner. At an earlier point he indicated that this mystery
had special importance for his Gentile readers (Col 1:27).
On the assumption that this is but a shorthand way of
speaking of the participation of Gentile believers in the
body of Christ on the same basis as those who were Jews
(which certainly is the meaning of the mystery of Christ

in the companion letter to the Ephesians—see 3:4-6), some students have concluded that a similar emphasis is intended here. "St. Paul might have been still at large, if he had been content to preach a Judaic gospel. It was because he contended for Gentile liberty, and thus offended Jewish prejudices, that he found himself a prisoner."[1] It is true, of course, that Jews made the seizure in the temple area (Ac 21:27-32). But it is also possible that "the mystery of Christ" is simply a synonym for the gospel in this passage, judging from the parallel passage in Ephesians 6:19, without any intentional stress on the equality of Jews and Gentiles in the body of Christ.

Intercession for an opening to proclaim the gospel is not the whole of Paul's concern. He wants to be sure that when the opportunity is provided (and he already had a broad promise from the Lord to encourage him in this respect— Ac 23:11) that he will not fail to take advantage of it (Col 4:4). To make the gospel *manifest,* to state it clearly, was just as much an obligation as the duty to bear witness. How could men be expected to believe if the word was not made understandable? That Paul was able to use his situation to good effect is clearly indicated by his recital of the events that followed in his letter to the Philippians (1:12-14).

CONDUCT TOWARD THE UNSAVED (4:5-6)

The theme continues to be basically the same, only now the witness of the readers is considered. Presumably, they are a minority in their community. They have no church building. They have no New Testament. They are without gospel tracts. How are they going to commend the gospel? Paul points to their *walk,* their daily conduct in

the sight of their fellows. He is saying that their conduct
can have a powerful evangelizing influence on the unsaved;
for, if these people see a type of life that is superior to their
own, the chances are good that they will want to inquire
after its secret. This will lead to conversation about Christ
and His saving work. When Paul calls for a Christian
"walk" that is characterized by "wisdom," he may well
have in mind that there are misunderstandings and prejudices about "the way" which need to be banished by up-
right, consistent conduct (see 1 Pe 2:12).

"Them that are without" is one of several expressions
used by Paul to describe the unsaved. In two passages (1
Th 4:12; 1 Ti 3:7) the value of making a good impression
on such people is spelled out and serves as a kind of commentary on our passage. Perhaps a little thought should be
given to the term *outsiders* (RSV). What does it suggest?
While it might be argued from 1 Corinthians 5:12-13
(RSV) that the term is used in a somewhat depreciatory
sense, this is probably a mistake, since nothing of this sort
is at all apparent in the other passages. Far from betoken-
ing an attitude of Pharisaic exclusiveness on the part of
those who used the term, it was both a lament and a challenge—a lament that those on the outside were not on the
inside and a challenge to keep the walk steady and consistent so that it might lead to discussion and ultimate
conversion.

That this is the correct interpretation is apparent from
what follows: "redeeming the time." This expression can
be more clearly stated as "eagerly buying up the opportunity," that is, capitalizing on every occasion to let one's
conduct speak for the high standards of Christian life and

thus bear testimony to Christ, who makes it possible (cf. Mt 5:16). Needless to say, there is not much room here for monastic seclusion as embodying the ideal for Christianity.

Still with an eye to possible contacts between believers and unsaved people, the apostle gives counsel to his readers about their speech or conversation (Col 4:6). It should "be always with grace." Although it is tempting to give *grace* its theological meaning, this is improbable here. More likely is the idea of beauty and winsomeness, such as that of our Lord, captivating those who listened (Lk 4:22). As in His case, there is no guarantee that those who hear will accept the content of the presentation, but at least attention is secured and a favorable atmosphere created for the communication of a witness. "Seasoned with salt" may well go a step further by suggesting that there should be a Christian flavor to the conversation, which should not be confined to insipid talk or mere platitudes but move to important matters that will invite the light which revelation can provide. The objective here is to cultivate a sensitivity to each individual, so as to be able to meet his objections and show how the gospel can supply his needs. The word *answer* suggests the possibility of considerable discussion about spiritual things. The thought moves in the orbit of 1 Peter 3:15.

COMMENDATION OF PAUL'S MESSENGERS (4:7-9)

The modern reader, in coming to this point in the letter, may tend to dismiss the closing remarks as being of far less interest than the teaching which has gone before. This is a natural tendency, but we should try to place ourselves in the position of those to whom Paul wrote. He is writing a letter, and in such a document personal items are eminently fitting and eagerly received. Gathered up in "all my state" (Col 4:7) are such personal items as his health, general situation, hopes, and prospects. The same expression ("my affairs," ASV) occurs in Ephesians 6:21, in a passage strictly parallel to this one. Luke uses the same Greek idiom when noting that Festus communicated to king Agrippa the things that had to do with Paul (Ac 25:14, "cause"), that is, the items that were involved in his case.

It is of interest to note that while Paul proposes to let Tychicus, the bearer of the letter, relate such things to the Colossians rather than include them himself, he did not follow this procedure in writing to the Philippians, probably a year or two later. Instead of committing such matters to Epaphroditus, his messenger, he related them himself (Phil 1:12-23). Two explanations can be offered for this. One is the fact that Paul felt very close to the Philippians and for this reason was able to speak freely of personal matters. Whereas the Colossians were largely strangers, the Philippians were his friends. He had founded the church and had visited it more than once at later periods. If the apostle had not included information about himself, the church would have been disappointed. A second reason is that Paul's affairs recorded in Philippians had a definite relation to the gospel and its progress in the Roman capital. Consequently he could the more conscientiously include them in a letter devoted to the interests of Christ his Lord.

The bearer of this letter was Tychicus, whose name means either fortuitous or fortunate. He had a similar role in relation to the Ephesian epistle (Eph 6:21-22). He belonged to the province of Asia and was probably

an Ephesian (Ac 20:4). Later on he may have been sent
by Paul to Crete to relieve Titus so that the latter might
leave to go to Paul (Titus 3:12). Still later (2 Ti 4:12)
Paul sent him to Ephesus from Rome, which presents
the possibility that he would help in the ministry there
while Timothy went to be with Paul as he faced martyr-
dom. Every reference to this man seems to involve being
a messenger. From Acts 20:4 it is evident that he was a
representative of the churches of the province of Asia,
charged with conveying their gifts to the poor saints at
Jerusalem. In view of all this, it was natural that Paul
would call upon him to take Colossians to its destination.
The only strange thing is that no greeting from him is included in the letter of Paul to Philemon, written and dis-
patched at the same time as Colossians. It is possible that
he and Philemon were not known to each other.

Tychicus clearly belonged to that circle of men who attached themselves to Paul and continued faithfully to serve
with him, never attaining great prominence but proving
invaluable as liaison figures between the apostle and his
churches. This reflects favorably on Paul, for his helpers
recognized in him a man of God fully dedicated to his task,
having a deep sense of divine mission, one who was worthy
of their assistance. Men who lack this deep sense of call
find it difficult to retain associates. Paul was an apostle, one
sent. Tychicus was his shadow, so to speak. Certainly he
is given high endorsement, for much the same commendation is accorded him as Epaphras (cf. Col 1:7). As "fellow-
servant," he was a partner with Paul in Christian work.

Continuing to dwell on the purpose of sending Tychicus,
the apostle includes this item: "that he might know your

estate" (Col 4:8). This is indeed the way some manuscripts have it, but the better text has "that you may know
how we are" (RSV). This makes better sense than the
other, for Paul would hardly send Tychicus all the way to
Colosse to find out how the believers were getting along
when Epaphras, who had just come from there, was available to provide such information. But Tychicus was to
have a ministry in Colosse beyond the assignment of delivering the letter. He was to "encourage" (RSV) the
hearts of the saints. Presumably the messenger will accomplish this goal by the news he brings of Paul and
Epaphras, also by his own experience of the Lord's saving
and preserving mercy.

Tychicus had a traveling companion in the person of
Onesimus, whose story, so far as we know it, is contained in
Paul's letter to Philemon. From the fact that the apostle
was able to say, "who is one of you" (v. 9), it can be inferred that he came from Colosse, which is confirmed by
the letter to Philemon, where the reception of the runaway
slave by his master is the theme. What is quite remarkable
is the way Paul describes him here, not simply as a "beloved brother" but also as a *faithful one*. Paul was obliged
to grant, in writing to Philemon, that Onesimus had been
unprofitable in the past. Evidently he had proved himself
to the apostle's satisfaction since his conversion. Although
the chief reason for sending Onesimus was to effect his
restoration by Philemon through the good offices of the
letter Paul wrote to this brother, Onesimus was to join
with Tychicus in telling what he knew about developments
in Paul's case and about his activities in the imperial city.

GREETINGS FROM PAUL'S COMPANIONS (4:10-14)

It was a rare thing for this man of action to be alone, as he was at Athens (Ac 17:15-16). Like a magnet he drew others to himself and made them his colaborers. Even in captivity he seems never to have been completely without associates, although his second experience of imprisonment at Rome was a severe test for his friends, posing a threat that they also might be condemned if they visited him (2 Ti 4:16-17). At the time he wrote Colossians, he could name half a dozen (not including the two who were leaving for the east) who were at his side.

First on the list is *Aristarchus*. Of five references to him in the New Testament, three are found in Acts. Two of the three label him a Macedonian (Ac 19:29; 27:2). Twice he is designated a man of Thessalonica. In the present passage he is called Paul's fellow prisoner, a description attached to three others in various places: Andronicus and Junias (Ro 16:7) and Epaphras (Phile 23). What does it mean? It is difficult to think that Paul is using figurative language here or in the other passages, as though to say that these men, like himself, have been taken captive by Christ to do His will. This would imply that he and they had been converted at the same time, which is not true. Accepting the literal sense as alone allowable, we can only conjecture how Aristarchus came to share Paul's lot. We know that he started out with Paul on the trip to Rome (Ac 27:2). Lightfoot may be right in concluding that Aristarchus left the ship at Myra, since it was turning west and he was headed for Macedonia.[2] Presumably he was free to do this because he was not a prisoner at that time.

Evidently he went to Rome later. Once there, he may have fallen under suspicion by the authorities, with the result that he was compelled to share Paul's captivity. The other possibility is that he voluntarily accepted the status of prisoner in order to be with Paul and aid him in various ways. "From the fact that here Aristarchus and not Epaphras is called a fellow-prisoner, while in Phm. 23 it is Epaphras and not Aristarchus who is so called, it has been conjectured that perhaps they took turns to share the quarters of the prisoner Apostle."[3]

Mark is the second man to be named. He is called "sister's son to Barnabas" (which would make him a nephew), but this translation in the KJV provides a meaning of the Greek original which is not attested until later. The current meaning was "cousin." The blood tie helps to explain Barnabas' devotion to Mark and his insistence on taking him along for a second time when Paul was unwilling to do so because Mark had deserted the missionary party on the first trip (Ac 13:13; 15:37-39). Mark is in Rome and evidently planning a trip to the east, so Paul takes pains to endorse him. A more outspoken commendation appears in 2 Timothy 4:11, where Paul states that he is useful to him for ministry. Lightfoot comments on the two passages, "The studious recommendation of St. Mark in both passages indicates a desire to efface the unfavourable impression of the past."[4] Nothing is known about the "commandments" Paul refers to or how they were communicated, but it is likely that they were intended to overcome hesitation on the part of believers in Asia to welcome a man who had become notorious as one who had put his hand to the plow and then looked back. That Mark eventually was restored to favor in the church universal is indicated by the tradition that he wrote the gospel which bears his name, with Peter as his chief source of information (see 1 Pe 5:13).

A third figure is *Jesus* who is called *Justus*. This second name not only distinguished him from Jesus of Nazareth but expressed his adherence to the law and traditions of the Jews. We know from Hegesippus' account of James the brother of our Lord that he was commonly called James the Just because of his Nazirite life and devotion to fasting and prayer.[5] Two others are noted as bearing this name: Joseph Barsabbas (Ac 1:23) and a man named Titius, a Corinthian (Ac 18:7, RSV). The latter reference is of interest because Titius was a God-fearer and a Gentile. He must have been intensely devoted to Judaism in his preconversion days in order to have earned his designation of Justus. However, in the case of the man who is being referred to by Paul, it is stated that he was "of the circumcision," hence a Jew like Mark. Aristarchus is apparently included, despite the fact that he had a Greek name. This was quite common in the Dispersion. Even some Palestinian Jews had Greek names (Ac 6:5).

These three were the *only men* among the circumcision at Rome whom Paul could acknowledge as his "fellowworkers unto the kingdom of God" (Col 4:11). Many Jewish Christians in the city were not sympathetic toward him. Light on this may be afforded by Philippians 1:15-17, where the apostle indicates that some carried on Christian testimony out of envy and rivalry, thinking to add affliction to his bonds. This was at a somewhat later time than the writing of Colossians, but opposition may have been developing by the time he sent this letter. Such people could

be called workers, perhaps, but certainly not his fellow
workers. Under such conditions, we can understand how
the three loyal figures were a real comfort to the apostle.
The mention of "the kingdom of God" invites comparison
with Paul's preaching in Rome as reported by Luke (Ac
28:31).

Epaphras is the next one to extend his greeting through
Paul (Col 4:12-13). Though little is known of this man,
the available information suggests that he was distinguished
by an unusual devotion to the Lord, to Paul, and to the
churches for which he was responsible. Paul already has
called him a faithful minister of Christ and a dear fellow
servant (1:7). Proof of his attachment to Paul appears in
his voluntary sharing of his friend's captivity in order to
provide him fellowship and assistance (Phile 23). To do
this doubtless meant a prolonging of his stay in Rome at a
time when his presence was needed at Colosse. In mentioning him, Paul adds the note, as he had done with Onesimus,
that he was a resident of Colosse. But he says a great deal
more, going on to describe Epaphras' intense concern for
the friends back home and his strenuous spiritual labor for
them by way of intercession. The Greek word used here
for "labouring fervently" is also rendered "fight" (Jn
18:36) and describes the athlete who contends with others
for the prize in the race ("striveth," 1 Co 9:25). Epaphras
seemed to be *always* occupied with this intense spiritual
wrestling with God on behalf of his converts. He poured
himself into it unsparingly.

The objective of this prayer warrior was that they might
"stand mature and fully assured in all the will of God"

(RSV). There were influences at work to make them waver in their original faith. They needed to be grounded anew in Christ (cf. 1 Co 16:13; Eph 6:13-14). To be mature the Colossian saints needed to take their stand on Christ and realize their completeness in Him, resisting any suggestion that worship of angels or ascetic practices are called for to make them acceptable to God. "Fully assured" implies a confidence that this stance is the right one and reflects the divine will in every respect.

The apostle is not quite through with his comments about Epaphras but insists on underscoring the intensity of his labor and its breadth as well, which extended to Christians in neighboring cities who may have been his converts also. *Zeal* does not adequately convey the meaning of the original. The rendering of the RSV, "he has worked hard," errs in giving a past reference to a verb which relates to the present. The idea is that Epaphras is expending painful toil upon his friends through his prayers. "Souls are precious in the sight of the pleader when for their sake he counts not the pain of such intercession too great a price to pay for their perfecting."[6] The inclusion of Laodicea and Hierapolis, cities of the Lycus valley only a few miles from Colosse, may be an indication that the same danger which was facing the Colossian church was recognized by Epaphras as a threat to the other communities.

Two others desire Paul to extend their greeting to the brethren at Colosse. They are *Luke* and *Demas* (Col 4:14). In the word *beloved* we can read Paul's personal attachment to this faithful friend Luke, who was at his side through much of his first captivity and again in the second (2 Ti 4:11). In identifying him as a physician, the apostle may be reflecting his own gratitude for the services of Luke in times of need. There is probably a connection between Paul's sickness on his first missionary journey (Gal 4:13) and his decision to have Luke join him on the second journey. Note how the physician makes his presence known in Acts 16:10 by shifting to the first person plural. He was more than a professional man, however. Since the "we" terminology ceases when Paul's movements take him beyond Philippi and resumes again when he returns to Philippi on his way to Jerusalem for the last time (Ac 20:1-6), the natural conclusion is that Luke remained in Philippi to direct the work there during this interval. No wonder Paul called him a fellow worker in Philemon 24. Added to all this is the contribution to the Christian cause of which moderns are most aware, the literary labors which provided for the church the gospel which bears his name and the book of Acts. It is impossible even to estimate the travel and research that were necessary in order to produce these records.

Demas was a man of different caliber. The contrast is seen in the poignant language Paul uses in his farewell epistle, written shortly before his death. Demas, out of love for this present world, had forsaken him. Luke alone remained with him (2 Ti 4:10 11). Like Luke, Demas seems to have been a Gentile (cf. Col 4:11) and apparently had his home in Thessalonica, since he made his way there after leaving Paul. The lack of any commendation in the passage before us may foreshadow the desertion that came later.

GREETINGS FROM PAUL (4:15-17)

The word *salute* is not different from *greet*, as they are one word in the original. Modern usage confines *salute* almost entirely to military custom, but its Latin derivation emphasizes solicitude for one's health or general welfare. The Greek word used here is equivalent in force to our "remember me to."

The person to be greeted could be either Nymphas, a man, or Nympha, a woman. To add to the confusion, some manuscripts have *their* house, others *his*, still others *her*. It is perhaps easiest to think of a woman in this connection, in view of the prominence of women in the early church, especially in the matter of making their homes available as a meeting place (Ac 12:12; 16:15, 40). A family formerly residing in Colosse may have moved to Laodicea and retained close ties with the saints at the former location. Some students favor the idea that this group actually resided at Hierapolis (cf. Col 4:13) on the ground that Paul would not slight believers there in this verse where he mentions those at Laodicea. But this is not conclusive, for Laodicea has been mentioned alone at an earlier point (2:1). Philemon, who was probably a resident of Colosse, since his slave Onesimus is so classified (4:9), had a group of believers meeting in his house (Phile 2). He is not singled out for a greeting, thus avoiding any appearance of favoritism. Archippus represented a special situation, as we shall see.

The house-church is a phenomenon noted at several points in the New Testament. Christians did not have church buildings until the third century. When official persecution ceased, building greatly increased. In small communities, one such group was probably adequate for the number of believers, but in the larger centers of population several were needed (Ro 16:5, 14, 15). The church today views this feature of early Christianity with great interest, for it seems to provide a model on which believers can meet in relatively small groups for fellowship and instruction while retaining connection with the congregation as a whole.

Included in these closing words of the apostle is instruction about the letter he is now bringing to a close. Naturally it will be read aloud to the congregation, but it is also to be passed on to "the church of the Laodiceans" for their edification (Col 4:16). The trouble that was infecting the Colossian church could easily spread to Laodicea, in which case the reading of the letter would bring a timely warning against the danger. But there is more to the directions of the apostle, for he requests the Colossians to see to it that a letter from Laodicea be obtained for reading in the assembly at Colosse. What does this mean? It does not mean that the letter emanated from this nearby city, as though it had been composed there, for Paul had not been there (2:1). It could refer to a letter drafted by Paul to Christians in that place, a letter which has since been lost. But if it had sufficient importance to be sent from Laodicea to Colosse, the chances of its being allowed to drop out of sight are slim. The most natural conclusion is that Paul is referring to the Ephesian epistle, which seems to have been intended for the churches of the province of Asia rather than for the church in Ephesus alone. This assumption rests on several considerations, one of which is that the

Ephesian letter contains no personal greetings from the apostle. Another is that our leading manuscripts lack the words *in Ephesus* at the beginning. Even though this letter resembles Colossians closely at many points, there is enough additional material to make it worthwhile that the believers in Colosse should have the benefit of hearing it read.

From the very beginning of his letter writing to churches, Paul was insistent that his communications be read to all of the saints (1 Th 5:27). It was a natural development that this practice should be extended to groups in nearby areas by having copies made and sent by the receiving church (2 Co 1:1). This was an important step in the formation of the New Testament, for on the analogy of synagogue practice, where only the Word of God was read, the churches were giving implicit recognition to Paul's letters as God's Word. If what he gave the congregations orally was worthy of being called the Word of God (1 Th 2:13) and his letters were written in lieu of words to be given orally if he were personally present, there is nothing strange about the process which finally resulted in the gathering together of Paul's writings and recognizing them as the word of God for the entire church.

A special communication for Archippus is reserved for the close of the letter (Col 4:17). In Philemon, written at the same time, this name appears, linked with those of Philemon and Apphia (Phile 2), making probable the assumption that he was their son. Paul calls him a fellow soldier. Here in Colossians he is recognized as having a ministry which he had "received in the Lord." Possibly he had accepted responsibility in the Colossian church for leadership when Epaphras found it necessary to leave for a season to visit Paul. The odd thing is that the apostle does not address him directly but only through the congregation. This may imply that he was still young and somewhat inexperienced. At any rate the charge to *fulfill* his ministry would remind him of the great demands of his mission and of the necessity of working in humble cooperation with the believers whom he was seeking to lead.

FAREWELL (4:18)

At this point, it seems, the apostle took the pen from the helper to whom he had been dictating. His greeting is appended in his own handwriting and his name is included. He adopted this plan as insurance against the forging of letters in his name (2 Th 3:17; cf. 2:2). "Remember my bonds" is his only parting request. Is this an indirect appeal to pray for his release? Or is it his way of inviting attention to the many sacrifices he has willingly made for Christ and the church, in the hope that his readers may be stirred to a comparable devotion? Nothing could bring him greater satisfaction.

As with all his letters, Paul brings this one to a close with the benediction of *grace* that suggests the truth of the longer and more formal statement of 2 Corinthians 13:14—"the grace of the Lord Jesus Christ . . . be with you all."

NOTES

CHAPTER 1

1. J. B. Lightfoot, *St. Paul's Epistles to the Colossians and to Philemon,* pp. 134-35.

2. Handley C. G. Moule, *Colossians Studies,* p. 53.

CHAPTER 2

1. Handley C. G. Moule, *Colossians Studies,* p. 78.
2. T. K. Abbott, *A Critical and Exegetical Commentary . . . Colossians,* p. 231.

CHAPTER 4

1. John Eadie, *A Commentary on the Greek Text . . . Colossians,* p. 175.
2. T. K. Abbott, *A Critical and Exegetical Commentary . . . Colossians,* p. 271.

CHAPTER 5

1. W. R. Nicholson, *Oneness with Christ,* p. 216.
2. Matthew Arnold *Obermann Once More.*
3. R. C. H. Lenski, *The Interpretation of St. Paul's Epistles to the Colossians, . . . and to Philemon* (Columbus, Ohio: Wartburg, 1956), p. 158.
4. W. Fairweather, *The Background of the Epistles* (New York: Scribners, 1935), p. 23.
5. Justin Martyr *Dialogue with Trypho,* chap. 28.
6. Thomas Chalmers, *The Expulsive Power of a New Affection* (New York: Thomas V. Crowell, 1901).

CHAPTER 6

1. A. T. Robertson, *Paul and the Intellectuals,* p. 175.
2. A. S. Peake, "The Epistle of Paul to the Colossians," p. 543.
3. F. W. Beare, "The Epistle to the Colossians," pp. 228-29.
4. John Eadie, *A Commentary on the Greek Text . . . Colossians,* p. 265.

CHAPTER 7

1. J. B. Lightfoot, *St. Paul's Epistles to the Colossians and to Philemon,* p. 231.
2. Ibid., p. 236.
3. L. B. Radford, *The Epistle to the Colossians,* p. 308.
4. Lightfoot, p. 237.
5. Hegesippus, as quoted by Eusebius *Ecclesiastical History,* 2.23.4-6.
6. H. S. Seeking, *The Men of the Pauline Circle* (London: Chas. H. Kelly, 1914), p. 153.

SELECTED BIBLIOGRAPHY FOR FURTHER STUDY

Abbott, T. K. *A Critical and Exegetical Commentary on the Epistles to the Ephesians and to the Colossians.* The International Critical Commentary. New York: Scribner's, 1902.

Beare, F. W. Introduction and Exposition to "The Epistle to the Colossians." In *The Interpreter's Bible,* vol. 11. New York: Abingdon, 1955.

Bruce, F. F. and Simpson, E. K. *Commentary on the Epistles to the Ephesians and the Colossians.* New International Commentary. Grand Rapids: Eerdmans, 1957.

Eadie, John. *A Commentary on the Greek Text of the Epistle of Paul to the Colossians.* 2d ed. Edinburgh: T. & T. Clark, 1884.

Lightfoot, J. B. *St. Paul's Epistles to the Colossians and to Philemon.* London: Macmillan, 1884.

Moule, C. F. D. *The Epistles of Paul the Apostle to the Colossians and to Philemon.* Cambridge Greek Testament Commentary. Cambridge: U. Press, 1957.

Moule, Handley C. G. *Colossian Studies.* 2d ed. London: Thynne, n.d.

Nicholson, W. R. *Oneness with Christ: Expository Lectures on the Epistle to the Colossians.* Chicago: Bible Inst. Colportage Assn., 1903.

Peake, A. S. "The Epistle of Paul to the Colossians." In *The Expositor's Greek Testament,* vol. 3. London: Hodder & Stoughton, n.d.

Radford, L. B. *The Epistle to the Colossians and the Epistle to Philemon.* Westminster Commentaries. London: Methuen, 1931.

Robertson, A. T. *Paul and the Intellectuals: The Epistle to the Colossians.* New York: Doubleday, 1928.

Thomas, W. H. Griffith. *Christ Pre-eminent: Studies in the Epistle to the Colossians.* Chicago: Bible Inst. Colportage Assn., 1923.

Wilson, R. McL. *Gnosis and the New Testament.* Philadelphia: Fortress, 1968.

———. *The Gnostic Problem.* London: Mowbray, 1958.

Moody Press, a ministry of the Moody Bible Institute, is designed for education, evangelization and edification. If we may assist you in knowing more about Christ and the Christian life, please write us without obligation to: Moody Press, c/o MLM, Chicago, Illinois 60610.